# For We Have This Treasure

# For We Have This Treasure

## The Yale Lectures on Preaching, 1943

PAUL SCHERER

**BAKER BOOK HOUSE**
Grand Rapids, Michigan

TO MY WIFE

Quantum mihi te sinuoso in pectore fixi

*Persius*

*Copyright 1944 by Harper & Brothers*
*Paperback edition issued 1976 by*
*Baker Book House*
*with the permission of the copyright owner*
*ISBN: 0-8010-8073-8*

PHOTOLITHOPRINTED BY CUSHING - MALLOY, INC.
ANN ARBOR, MICHIGAN, UNITED STATES OF AMERICA
1976

# Contents

v

O Beauty on the darkness hurled,
Be it through me you shame the world.

JOHN MASEFIELD
"Invocation," *Collected Poems*
The Macmillan Company

ᒐᒐᒐᒐᒐᒐᒐᒐᒐᒐᒐᒐᒐ *Preface* ᒐᒐᒐᒐᒐᒐᒐᒐᒐᒐᒐᒐᒐ

These lectures grew originally out of a period of enforced silence when the moratorium declared on my speaking both public and private by certain kindly physicians left me with leisure which I thought could most profitably be spent in setting down on paper much that I had got from others in this high art and sacrament of preaching, together with such observations of my own as had come to me over the lapse of some twenty years in the ministry.

In their first form they were delivered at the Lutheran Theological Seminary in Gettysburg, Pennsylvania, on the foundation of the Doctor and Mrs. Jeremiah Zimmerman Lectureship. During the five or six years that have followed, they have inevitably grown somewhat in girth if not in stature; and have been variously given at the Northfield General Conference, the Lutheran Theological Seminary at Mt. Airy, Philadelphia, Union Theological Seminary in New York, the Eden Theological Seminary in St. Louis, and the Theological Seminary at Hartford, Connecticut. Revised, and to a not inconsiderable extent rewritten, they were delivered as the Lyman Beecher Lectures at Yale Divinity School in April, 1943. With scarcely any change in form they are now offered for publication, but with no little hesitancy. My only hope is that they may prove of some measurable service to those who like myself feel continually drawn to a task that at once beckons and defeats, heartens and intimidates them.

It is perhaps assumed altogether too often that whoever accepts an invitation to lecture on this foundation or that thereby does implicitly if not overtly acknowledge and confess, as the liturgy has it, albeit without the lament, his own imagined fit-ness for the appointed duty. I dare say nothing could be wider of the mark. He may well be most useful to others who is himself most familiar with the difficulties, who has never discovered a way around them, whose going is still in the midst of them. As ministers of the gospel of Jesus Christ in an age as crucial as any through which humanity has passed, all of us must know ourselves to be almost equally unqualified actors standing at the heart of the most thrilling drama of history, which is the Word forever being made flesh; and where none can be adequate, it may surely and properly belong to each of us to share with others as much knowledge as we have won of aids and perils, of methods and goals, if so be that out of the common store of life's changing fortunes may come wisdom.

What is said in these pages, as will be evident at a glance, is intended frankly and primarily for ministers. And yet I am not wholly without the desire, secretly cherished, that there may be others here and there who in leafing through them will find some help and encouragement as they set about their own stewardship of "God's varied grace." That all may know whence and whither and by way of what, let me say that I begin in Chapter I with an attempt at orientation in this defeated and bewildered world which is both our heritage and the work of our hands, adding in a preliminary sort of way a few, at least, of the corollaries which have to be taken into account as to the manner of our approach to it if we are to be in any sense the agents of God's healing and creative purpose. The second chapter deals with the growing venture as we come steadily toward it, like horizons falling away from wind-swept heights, back and back upon each other, a panorama for every man or woman who wills to share our stern emprise, living out its demands, and so realizing its promises. Chapter III aims at a deliberate re-appraisement of the weapons of our spiritual warfare, an indication of the content and nature of the Chris-

tian gospel,—its doctrine of God and man, and the relationship
between the two in Jesus of Nazareth. The fourth has to do
more with the application of that gospel to our present situation,
and with the vibrant mood and reverent temper which must
mark its handling. The two last chapters are no doubt more
technical. They concern themselves, the one with the sources of
ideas, with the gathering of material and the organization of
thought; the other with writing, with style and clarity and
color, and with the goal of it all in free utterance. The whole is
the story of a kind of pilgrimage, and of little moment other
than to those companions of the way who fare on, but not too
well, and never far!

The bulk of it has been set down bodily within a kind of
ready-made framework lifted here and there from Paul's
epistles; and that because I have been continually impressed, all
along the road, with the appropriateness of his counsel, both
direct and contingent, to all and sundry who would essay to be
not disciples only but ambassadors of the Word. The so-called
"form criticism," some of which would re-address most of his
letters and have them coming from the church instead of to it,
has not disturbed me much in the process. Whether we are
listening in them to the experienced genius of a fiery little
apostle or to the conglomerate genius of the early Christian
community, it is yet genius; and against it as against a vast
screen moves the stirring panorama of a titanic struggle. There
are *dethroned powers* and *minds grown dark*. There are *men
with glad, good news, branded* on their body *with the owner's
stamp of Jesus*. There is *the story of the cross,* which is God's
brave *Yes in Christ*. There is *the favour of suffering,* and the
*deep concern* of one who is *less than the least of all saints,* an
*illustration of Christ's utter patience,* yet a *workman sound* and
unashamed of *the way he handles the word of Truth,* pressing
*on to the goal*. I am possessed of no better vehicle for saying

what needs saying, what I at least need to hear, if I too am to make *my little boast* of the *God who has chosen things which are not to put down things that are*. It is almost as if Paul himself were standing this hour in front of us, looking at what we see, telling us what he has found, having come that way.

Of my indebtedness to others I hardly know how to speak. I shall try to indicate it as I go along, so much of it at least as is now traceable. Certain it is that I have drawn from many sources, and some forgotten; but where memory fails there is still gratitude. To the Faculty of Yale Divinity School, for the invitation extended to me; to Dean Weigle, for his gracious courtesy and helpful suggestions; to Dean Brown, to Dr. Halford Luccock and Dr. Richard Niebuhr for much which they themselves through the years have been unaware of giving; to the professors and students and alumni for their hospitality and considerate attention—to all of them I would make this acknowledgement of lasting obligation. To Dr. James Moffatt for the stimulus and flashing insights of his translation of the Bible, of which I have made use throughout except as otherwise indicated. To Mrs. Gladys Olds Anderson for her assiduous search through many volumes in the checking of references that I fear are all too frequent. To the congregation of the Lutheran Church of the Holy Trinity in New York, which has been so patient with me so long. And to those not least but last who have made for me all the while the constant happiness of a home. *What more shall I say? Time would fail me to tell.*

❧ ❧

Blind! Blind! that demands the useful and sees not that ever thence life becomes more useless!

LEOPARDI

✦✦✦✦✦✦✦✦✦✦✦✦✦✦✦✦✦✦✦✦✦✦✦✦✦✦✦✦✦✦✦✦✦✦✦✦✦✦✦✦✦✦✦✦✦✦

# Chapter 1

## A CONSTANT PAGEANT

✦✦✦✦✦✦✦✦✦✦✦✦✦✦✦✦✦✦✦✦✦✦✦✦✦✦✦✦✦✦✦✦✦✦✦✦✦✦✦✦✦✦✦✦✦✦

### INTRODUCTION

There is no reason at all to suppose that in this, the seventy-first year of the Lyman Beecher Lectureship, anything new or original can be added to what has already been said about preaching by men who have been both masters and ornaments of their craft. It is written that long ago in the fields of Boaz the young men were commanded concerning Ruth, saying, Let fall some of the handfuls of purpose for her, and leave them, that she may glean them, and rebuke her not (Ruth 2:16, A.V.). Such knowledge as I have of the sixty and more books which constitute the series of published lectures on this foundation has not led me to conclude that any such merciful spirit has gone before! The fields have all too adequately been raked and swept. The grain has all too skillfully been gathered into barns. The only course possible for me, at least, if I am to address myself to this subject, is to assume that "what is valuable is not new"; that "the new is but the old come true"; and that what has been alive may be alive again, tingling once more with urgency, taking on warmth and color interminably for having passed through the medium of yet another's mind and heart.

And who will say that here is not one of the many high functions which such a Lectureship may serve? Calling in from time to time not always a Joshua but now and then a kind of Caleb, back from Canaan, returned for a moment from searching out the land, its mountains and passes, its valleys and rivers, bringing only that eager word to go up and possess it; or possibly as this or that man-at-arms might come from the gallant tumult of the Holy Wars to bespeak of all men everywhere high courage and lives disposed to instant peril in this greatest of all great enterprises, "the world-winning or world-losing wagers and commitments" of the Christian gospel. Undoubtedly there will be much of what I shall have to report that will be itself a kind if preaching. Let me be bare-faced about it and unashamed. I have never learned the secret of pursuing a vocation while leaving at home as much of it as is possible. If along the way I draw too largely, and even more largely than that, on my own experience, it is simply because I have nothing else which is really mine. Robert Benchley once wrote a book which he called his *Ten Years in a Quandary;* and I have been in this over twice as long. It should be doubly useful. And that before anything else is my sober purpose. Some half-hearted effort has indeed been made to reduce the number of my "personal appearances," together with the pronouns that herald them, but without appreciable result. I know now that, wrestle as I might, the *I*'s would still be too closely set. My plea is only for that measure of confidence which you may achieve in spite of them.

For your encouragement, however, I add that we shall make our journey from place to place at least within sight of one other whom God chose to be His most valiant spokesman in a time strangely like our own. Nobody could sit down, as I did again not long ago, and read straight through the letters of St. Paul, especially in the translation which Dr. Moffatt has given us, without realizing how much of what is said there sounds like the penetrating whisper of some ardent fellow-traveler who knows even in the dark each turn of the road. On almost every page what I had in mind to write turned out to have been written for me centuries gone; and I found myself not reading so much as listening with a certain amazement, intently, too, for your sake and for my own,—as if here were one who was actually doing this thing that I am trying to do—, growing more and more confident as I went on that he should be allowed to do it.

Let me set down now but one thing more: that I have had the keenest pleasure in anticipating these hours with you and in trying to get ready for them. As I have had to look back over my own course, I have been increasingly mindful of that Other Will which means so intensely and means good, until I have grown not a little envious of your youth, and of its freshness as it faces that untried future which comes so steadily on to meet you; wishing more than once that I too might stand at the threshold again with the zest I have today,—by how many odds greater than ever it was before!—for this "open secret" of God in Christ. There have been disappointments enough, and failures, naturally, moods of bitterness and resentment, of bewilderment and frustration. But I have found that they need never get much of a foothold anywhere. Always there is a kind of deep content which keeps pushing its way back. Paul called it the peace of God and said it was like a garrison (Philippians 4:7), shoving that troublesome brood over the edge, disengaging their fingers as they try to cling on, and brushing its hands at last to be rid of them down there in the abyss where they be-

long. The most commanding thing I have learned is just this
relish, this taste and tang of life, with the immemorial figure of
a Galilean in the center of it, waging his hungry, stubborn
hopes. I ask merely that you allow me to savour it again with
you.

Our story, then, begins with what the apostle calls

My Divine Commission*

*as a priest of Christ . . .
in the service of God's gospel.* It was this sense of high appointment that undergirded him all his way along. It sent him back
to the stones at Lystra. It filled him with a passion that turned
as at a signal now into some desperate entreaty, now into a
hymn of gratitude. Here is some quick severity, there an eager
tenderness. Over and over again are sentences that pay no attention to grammar, with the words tripping on one another's
heels, piling up into a kind of chaos, with the light of God on it,
the gallant sunshine of His soul. If I could only clear these win-
dows of mine to let it through! *Wherever I go,* he writes after
the trouble he had had with the church at Corinth, *God makes
my life*

A Constant Pageant†

The whole procession
of the days—peril, shipwreck, hunger, thirst—moves along some
Via Sacra, brilliant and full of color. Nothing drab about any
of it!

Perhaps, with such an end in view, we should at the very start
clear out of the road all the nonsense we have picked up if any
in the matter of the call to the Christian ministry. There is such
a call; and when it comes, it comes straight from God. I believe
with all my heart that a man must hear it and feel its imperious
constraint before he can ever give himself with any whole-

* Romans 15:15, 16.
† II Corinthians 2:14.

hearted devotion and abiding wonder to this stewardship of the gospel. But I believe, too, that more than one minister has been confused by many of the things he has been taught about it and by a great deal that he has read. As a result, there are times when he begins to suspect the validity of whatever call he once felt himself to have had. He wonders if, after all, he too is not one of those prophets who ran, though not sent, who prophesied though the Lord had not spoken (*Jeremiah 23:21*); and that plays utter havoc with his work. He cannot go on with any peace or with any power if he questions long the very fact of his own vocation. He comes upon such a passage as this:

I would affirm my conviction that, in all genuine callings to the ministry, there is a sense of the divine initiative, a solemn communication of the divine will, a mysterious feeling of commission, which leaves a man no alternative but sets him in the road . . . a servant and instrument of the eternal God.[1]

And my hypothetical minister wonders pretty much what it is all about. His experience has been far less rotund and far less intangible. If this is what it means to be called, then—God knows—maybe it's all to do again.

Certainly, the only way out for such a one is to have somebody disabuse his mind, as promptly and as forcefully as may be, of all pious verbiage about mysterious voices and unforeseen events and occult influences and strange answers to prayer. These things of themselves cannot constitute the proper ground for any deep choice of the apostolic life. The conversion of Paul on the way to Damascus is not to be taken as the type of God's dealing with those whom He summons into His service as ambassadors of His truth. Amos may not be forgotten, with his long brooding on the social injustices of his day. Isaiah may not be forgotten, with his sudden consciousness in the midst of national catastrophe that the great God wanted another man. Jeremiah may not be forgotten, with his reluctant answer to that pressure which had kept growing within him until it seemed the culmination of an age-old purpose: "Before thou camest forth out of the womb, I sanctified thee and ordained thee a prophet"; and James and John may not be forgotten, or Matthew and Peter with the face they saw, and the presence that would not let them go, the love that haunted them down the dreary roads and set them apart for the gospel of God (Romans 1:1).

The voice of the Lord calling laborers into His harvest is as varied as human life itself, as manifold as the endless pattern of the fields and the clouds. It comes to every living soul by every conceivable channel. They are the apostles who hear and, not for any gain of theirs but for the gain of God and the world, whisper back, "Here am I; send me." Never on earth would I even attempt to discount the reality of those mystic assurances which come to some of us and make us so confident of our mission. But *I beseech you, brethren, by the mercies of God* (Romans 12:1, A.V.) let no man presume upon them; or decry his own uneventful experience of God's grace, as though no effective ministry could ever possibly be built upon such a tame and almost casual matter of fact.

Fundamentally—and this we must understand if we are to get clearly in our minds what I, at least, believe to be the true nature of this call to the ministry of the Gospel—, fundamentally, the preacher's chief function is to keep alive and cogent on this earth that awareness of Almighty God which is the soul's own creaturely response to its Creator. He is to open men's minds to the splendor that shines forever on the face of human life; to the beauty and the mystery of godliness; to the horses and chariots of fire that range themselves about this beleaguered place. He is to throw wide the door of every narrow room and let in the mountain and the sea. He is to hold all hearts everywhere quiet under the creative spell of the Infinite.

There is a story which I believe Lynn Harold Hough tells somewhere of a clerk, sitting on his high stool at a worn desk in a dingy corner, the columns of figures marching past him down the page ceaselessly. But he is a man of wider horizons than you think and of a more chivalrous spirit. There in front of him is a window, and in its stained glass at the top the mounted figure of a knight in armor setting out against all manner of tyranny in defense of innocence and righteousness and peace. And ever and again the pen of the little clerk would be lifted from the row of endless figures; the stooped shoulders would straighten for a moment, and in his eyes a light would gleam as they fixed themselves once more on what had become for him the symbol of his own fair and gallant quest, riding a clean course toward the City of the Most High.

Well, it is this that the preacher must do. He is to remind us in our common life of "the divine gleam that rests continually upon the sod." He is to help heaven come and dwell somewhere on the earth. And it is precisely his zest for this, his solemn eagerness himself to stand on the threshold of God's two worlds of sense and spirit, and there, under the quiet hand of the Master of Life, to interpret for all that will hear him what there is about living that is most firmly true and most deeply real,—it is just this that constitutes the workaday human aspect of his divine vocation. Let's look at it in some perspective.

The world into which Paul came was a strangely defeated and sobered world. He came, as we have come, at one of the greatest turning points in the story of human life. You will remember how in his letter to the Romans he seems suddenly to face about, looking sharply at them to make sure. *You know,* he says,

## What This Crisis Means

*It is far on in the night, the day is almost here* (Romans 13:11, 12). So does he give us his reading of current history. He is telling the hour by God's sundial, as he watches the shadow of eternity fall across the shifting surface of man's uneasy existence. It is clear to him that the end of an era has come. The ancient hope of God's people is about to be realized. What seemed distant is near at hand. Through eleven chapters he surveys the vast proportions of that divine imperative which we call Providence, as it arches over the whole earth. In the twelfth he sets about bringing it to one focus after another on the salient features of his immediate landscape. Obsessed with "the eternal antiquity of the truth," he sharpens it to its prompt and urgent bearing. No intimate detail of the familiar scene but is repeatedly illumined by his sweeping searchlight, around and around the horizon; while ever and again, keeper as he is of "the awful and mysterious Word of God," the beam swings up and down unceasingly between heaven and earth.

Some such service as that it is ours too to render, preachers or no preachers. As he was, so are we, interpreters within history of that which is not only within but above it. Once more in our time the movement of men and of nations has become a problem for theology. Again people want to know, in terms of God as well as of man, what it is all about. What kind of Deity is He Who allows this to happen? And what does it mean in the long story of human existence? Or does it have any meaning? We are beginning to suspect that the Bible was right: that the swift epic of our life is not one thing and God another. May it not be that the two are inseparably bound together? Not of course in the sense that one can argue from the things that happen to the wisdom and the power that make them happen. It is never possible for us to know God better through some medium which we have assumed to be more tangible than He. But in the sense that to believing minds the very flux of existence, as the Greeks viewed it, is far more revealing than the physical order of the universe; that it's no flux at all, but the determined shaping of some process in which we play a part, though only a part, while God holds it steadily on toward His inflexible purpose.

This it was that weighed so heavily on Paul.[2] It weighed heavily on every one of the prophets of Israel before him, and on all the evangelists and apostles. Not in doctrine did these men find their incentive. They found it in what to them was the story of God's dealing with human life. To their composite insight more than to anything else, so another has well said, we owe our very idea of history, not simply as something we do but also as something done to us. Surely the face of that history can be no less than our critical concern, as it was theirs. What if across it, in letters which run as deep as human need and stand as high as human destiny, were written today a strange new sense of the relevance of the Christian gospel!

For over a hundred years now historians and philosophers have been trying to see our disordered present in its proper perspective along the course of the centuries. Oddly enough they are almost unanimously agreed that for any adequate understanding of man's inner unhappiness which, having festered so long, is coming rapidly to a head, we shall have to turn back at least as far as the apostolic age. The writers of the New Testament were confronted on the stage of history with what to them seemed the vindication in judgment of God's sovereignty over an order that save for a few fitful stirrings of superstition here and there had left Him out of the picture and gone off to manage its own affairs. Existence for hundreds of years, through all the later phases of the Greek culture, had been integrated as well as it could be around itself, in a flat and two-dimensional world. Full of movement and becoming, it was yet hauntingly tragic, plunging along toward self-defeat, unmindful of eternity, and running at last straight into this Word of God which struck across it on the fields of Bethlehem in the crisis of which the apostle is here so vividly conscious. In the white-hot fires of persecution, during the years that followed, was wrought that fusion between the Greek tradition on the one hand and the Hebrew-Christian tradition on the other which still constitutes potentially at least our richest single inheritance. From it the stately structure of medieval Catholicism began to grow, with its solemn creeds and stately ritual, its towering Gothic arches and its slender spires, giving men their purchase again, a sort of fulcrum beyond themselves, as if they had "one foot in heaven." Human life seems to need that, if things down here are even to hold together! The creative impulse which it imparted to history is not even yet exhausted. For a thousand years, singlehanded and alone, it provided a crude and emergent Western civilization with a deep and underlying sense of community in the Body of Christ, which was the fellowship of the Christian church; and by means of its constant reference to another world it equipped the unlettered hordes of Europe with a meaningful outlook upon their life in this.

But always the pull of the years seems weighted on the side of the ancient and pagan past. From the twelfth to the sixteenth century life kept tipping over steadily toward ruin. The end came in those two great movements with which modern history begins, the Renaissance and the Reformation. They were both magnificent epics. It is a pity we should have twisted them into this Pandora's box of fiendish mischief-making which has helped to wreck our world. The one, man-centered and two-dimensional, was bent on perpetuating and developing the classical strain in medieval culture, with a passionate faith in human progress. It found its mainspring in freedom of thought, and, like Faust, science-haunted and frenzied with dreams of power, betook itself to the deliberate exploitation of everything under heaven. The other was God-centered and three dimensional. Its length and its breadth were at first mere corollaries of its height. Its freedom was freedom of conscience, and its only passionate hope was the hope of redemption. The debacle of our present age is the measure of their separate failure.[3]

For a while, but not for long, the Reformation was able to hold in check the headlong career of the Renaissance toward chaos; at last with an almost unconditional surrender it has had to yield. Man by exalting himself has finally become the puppet and the pawn of his own success.[4] The child of nature has triumphed over the child of God and has found in the triumph his own inexorable defeat. Life in two dimensions has come off with all the garlands, and they are withered. In its long rebellion against authority, in the violent assertion of its own mastery, it has cleared from the field both God and the human soul, to wander now among the ruins. Wrote Milton Mayer in the Saturday Evening Post:[5]

The civilization which stemmed in Greek philosophy, and towered high in medieval cathedrals, has flowered in department-stores. The ends of life have become the goods of the body. Existence has been turned into a continuous bank-run; and the bank is now closing.

That, I submit to you, is what crisis means.[6] It means that when an order has become thoroughly secularized it has committed suicide. It means that the Kingdom of God is not a by-your-leave or an if-you-please; it is still a Kingdom, and to rebel against it is to pay the price of treason. *For God ranks*
This World's Wisdom*

*as "sheer folly." It*
*is written He seizes the wise in their craftiness, and again, The*

* I Corinthians 3:19, 20.

*Lord knows the reasoning of the wise is futile.* In one realm after another human life has been able to do little more ultimately than to stultify itself. For the last four hundred years it has been investigating its world emptier and emptier, not at all as a result of the amazing insights which have been achieved through scientific discovery, but by reason of the arrogant conclusions which have been so gratuitously drawn from the facts. Somebody one day learned about evolution; and almost everybody the next day began to fraternize in a passion of self-abasement with the crystal and the clod. A few turned with fresh zeal to the study of astronomy; and straightway for the many the planet which is their home lost caste, and heaven disappeared in a table of logarithms. One took up physics, and three more offered to reproduce *urbs et orbis* in the laboratory the scheme of things entire. Psychology waved its wand, and the public was forthwith convinced that its soul had been transformed into a knee-jump. Conscience was dug up out of God and replanted in society, where it did not do so well.

On the surface of that witches' brew, where men kept busily stirring their own baseless assumptions into a cauldron-full of metaphysical absurdities, there appeared like scum a kind of "relativity" in morals, which immediately as in Plato's Greece began to spatter its sophistry over everything both public and private. Step by step people were driven to live on the rapidly diminishing ethical capital of their forebears; and step by step they became more thoroughly incapable of reproducing it. The wealth of self-immolating knowledge they had built up, often indiscriminate, rarely ever integrated, was taken over bodily into their so-called "systems of education," *until,* writes Paul,

Their Ignorant Minds Grew Dark *

You might almost think he had got wind of it. *The time will come,* he warns

* Romans 1:21.

Timothy *when people . . . will give up listening to the Truth and turn to myths. And their doctrine spreads like a gangrene* (II Timothy 4:3, 4; 2:17). Nobody any more, so we were told in our philosophically bankrupt and illiterate world, could possibly know things as they are. The universe was without ends. There was no abiding reality. Ideas were the steam given off by experience when it boiled. Nothing was changeless but change. "Down with absolutes." And to that "profane jargon," I am reliably informed, fifty per cent of the professors in the more outstanding of our American schools for the training of teachers subscribed.[7]

In such a desolation of freedom there seemed nothing to do but to relegate religion to the sphere of individual opinion. The framework of politics and economics was the only framework left within which men could discover for themselves some semblance of unity and fashion for themselves the shelter of a "real" world. But the same stubborn fatality was forever hard on their heels. Machines crowded in upon them. All their business was organized for profit. What production they could manage was geared with an eye to prices. The naive thrusts and balances of their capitalistic system kept breaking down. Millions were thrown out of employment. Until government itself became largely a device for giving people what they wanted. By little and little humanity's only defense against annihilation seemed to be Nietzsche's myth of the superman; its only defense against the meaninglessness of life, a monstrous collectivism which was promptly bolstered by a spurious creed and adorned with a spurious ritual. Whereupon the nations set about their age-old project of killing again. Having willed for their hunger nothing but bread, men brought upon themselves famine and death. By their own autonomous way they had arrived at their goal in an unblushing irrationality, the very ecstasy of negation, the demonism of frustration, personal and social. "Where there is no God, there is no man."[8]

This it seems to me is what we face, all of us alike. The aspect of it which commands me and takes me captive appears in the simple fact that "contemporary history has refuted contemporary culture." That is what got hold of Paul. There was more; but there was that. It was clear as a pikestaff to him that the world's resources were played out and God's were not. It was the gospel that needed no apology. Christianity had no rivals left. The powers that ruled the world were

### Dethroned Powers*

It was God's *mysterious wisdom, decreed from all eternity,* that was on the verge of coming inevitably into its own. He says it and shouts it and sings it. There are times when he seems to put a trumpet to his lips. After that it is organ music.

I see no reason why we today should be wearing any wet blankets. We need no defense. We need a message. And nothing has hurt that. It would appear that "the acids of modernity" have been eating their way not so much into the Christian religion, as Mr. Lippmann thought, but into the substitutes for it by which humanity has been trying its best to live. Who is left now to champion democracy as the panacea of all the ills that flesh is heir to? Here of late we have achieved a fresh devotion to it; but only romanticists believe any longer in its magic potency. We shall hardly do again what one author did in the roaring twenties: set down The Kingdom of Heaven in the index, and under it, See Democracy. Few are willing to assume in our time that "the American way of life" can be put into immediate operation anywhere by the quick device of military occupation and fiat. We are not so sure that we ourselves can be safely trusted with it. And more important than anything else, we are coming to realize that if any of it is going to function at

* I Corinthians 2:6.

all it has to be bound up far more closely than we ever dreamed with both the theological and the moral fabric of Christianity. Its fundamental principles are not solely the outgrowth of pagan law and pagan philosophy and pagan ethics. They are not solely the product of eighteenth century rationalism and optimism. They have flowered in the good earth of the Christian faith. They have been unbelievably shaped by it and colored by it; and they cannot now be torn free to carry on their life alone without its benefit and without its sanction.

In the realm of science the same insistent scepticism has been at work. The popular mind-set of the last century that has not wanted our brains to function unless they could dissect something or put it into a test tube has been corroded and loosened. Its hard and dogmatic pretensions on the subject of what is ultimately real in this universe have been cracked wide open by the newer physics. There appears to be more now in a Bach fugue than "drawing the tail of a dead horse across the entrails of a dead cat." Without offering any contribution to the writing of the play, says C. E. M. Joad,[9] scientists have themselves cleared the boards for religion by running a line through many of our erstwhile superstitions. Some of these may linger on for a while, the common-sense view of the world being usually a petrified version of the science of fifty years ago; but they are doomed: the revolution has already taken place.

So is it also with humanism: that attempt to deal with man as man, by which multitudes of us have been trying to live and which always results in dealing with man as less than he is. Today the cankerworm is busy at the heart of it. Not the ground on which Christianity stands,—man's utter helplessness to save himself, his imperative need of resources beyond his own —but the ground on which humanism has been attempting to stand, calls for re-examination, cries out for re-assessment. There is something devilishly stubborn about the way "progress" refuses to work, and "perfection" declines to put in an appearance. Evil has extended instead of reducing its limits. It begins to seem likely that, as nature can be understood only in that frame of reference which is man, so man, with his almost infinite possibilities in both directions, up and down, and this constant tension in his soul between them, can be understood only in that frame of reference which is God.[10] Our life shows too many symptoms of another life that impinges on it, presses in against it from every side, rattles the shutters it tries to close, knocks at its doors, and turns the knob. We are impossible conundrums without it, answerless riddles.

And so I say, who knows but that driven out of our ruined Edens we are actually crossing today the threshold of an era, centuries long it may be, when there shall be wrought out, not without suffering, it may be not without catastrophe, a new synthesis between the divided halves of our age-old inheritance; when the spirit of man shall once again, because humbly under God, lift tall with its rightful heritage, sacrificing none of its gains, but centering them where they have to be centered: its brave and stubborn hopes shaped by a will that is braver still and more stubborn; its deep and dark condition matched only by that other who holds in his scarred and steady hands the swinging movement of the years! Life is beginning, by the very judgments that weigh on it, to make sense again. History seems to be bearing its own witness; and that witness runs: *Thy testimonies, O Lord, have become exceeding credible.*

This call, then, to the Christian ministry does not come in a vacuum; not apart from the world, but in the closest conceivable relation with it. Distraught as that world was, and frightened, with hands everywhere held out, Paul could not for the life of him leave it alone.

## I Owe a Duty*

Here is not merely the pressure of a compassionate nature; it is the pressure within of a holy and compassionate God.

> Only like souls I see the folk thereunder,
>> Bound who should conquer, slaves who should be
>> kings,—
> Hearing their one hope with an empty wonder,
>> Sadly contented with the show of things;—
> Then with a rush the intolerable craving
>> Shivers throughout me like a trumpet call,—
> Oh to save these! to perish for their saving,
>> Die for their life, be offered for them all![11]

He is like a strong swimmer standing on the brink with the shout of a drowning man in his ears. No need to wait longer. There is a will moving in upon him, meditated from without by that crying which seems to fill the whole earth; and it is that will above all else that he heeds—beyond the urgency of every human situation, the call of all God's heaven to meet it. Let him who answers clear in the grace of our Lord Jesus Christ, in the love of God, and in the fellowship of the Holy Ghost (II Corinthians 13:14),—let him be God's man and Christ's apostle! Let him, trained and set to his appointed duties in the Christian church, be the herald of that act which is the Christain gospel, done from eternity in time, for us men and for our salvation. As the years unfold and he looks back, he will know who it was that spoke in his sure response to the stir and agony of human hearts. He will see how he was most divinely hedged about and compelled to it, in and through and above all things; until, staring wide-eyed at the life around him, he began on that day long since, and must needs now more than ever continue, to cry aloud in the silent reaches of his own soul, *Woe to me if I do not!* (I Corinthians 9:16).

* Romans 1:15.

I suggest now that we ask more particularly of the character and scope of his duties, trying to sketch them in as well as we can against this moving panorama of a baffled generation. What is the nature of our "Divine Commission"? Primarily it is a commission to preach. And to preach not just sermons, but that event in history and in eternity by which God entered most fully and effectively into human life. It is a commission to announce the good news of His Kingdom, bearing witness to that saving activity which is in Christ and of which the very bearing of the witness is itself a part. You will recall with what feeling Paul puts it (Romans 10:14): *How are they to invoke One in whom they do not believe? How are they to believe in One of whom they have never heard?*

How Are They Ever to Hear

*without a preacher?*

This it is which has always stood firmly at the center of the Christian religion. Someone has pointed out that Hinduism lives by ritual and social organization, Buddhism by meditation, Confucianism by a code of manners; but Christianity lives by "the foolishness of preaching" (I Corinthians 1:21, A.V.). So has it always been. The most creative and critical ages of its history—the ages of Paul and the apostles, of Ambrose and Augustine, of Urban, of Luther and Calvin and Wesley and Brooks—all of these have been the great ages of Christian preaching. Not just life or action or example or personal influence, but preaching. And so shall it ever be: until the Truth, which is God's "inescapable claim" upon us, ceases to come through personality; until He himself ceases to speak with human lips; until the love of Christ ceases to be the endless peril and the never-failing refuge of the human soul.

It follows therefore at once that the first business of the preacher is to assign to preaching in his own thought and in his practice the dignity that belongs to it. We owe that to the disillusioned and melancholy temper of the age. If something has to be done indifferently, let it be something else. A man's best may not be very good—that is not his fault; but anything less than his best when he stands before his congregation is scarcely more than an impertinence. To him who under the growing pressure of life's swift current holds his pulpit in some respect and his people with it, preaching comes first; and because preaching *takes* time, he *makes* time—which is the only way I know to *have* time. Makes it without scruple, deliberately and arbitrarily refusing to be caught among the wheels that turn the cranks, or by any crank that turns the wheels, of our often too elaborate church machinery; thrusting aside every enticing expedient so frequently adopted in order to lure passers-by into the fold, from church socials, with what Phillips Brooks used to call their "familiar but feeble odor of a cup of tea," to interdenominational programs and welfare work—from those multifarious and omnipresent guilds and organizations, fully half of which are as likely as not to be little more than "incorporated death," to the seemingly harmless printing of bulletins: scrapping it all if it interferes with his giving of his best to this task which of all his tasks is foremost.

You will not misunderstand me. Every one of these things which come clamoring for our attention may well have its value and its place. I only know that a man has to cut ruthlessly through them at times to get at the heart of his ministry, which is this living, moving, throbbing Word of God. I remember a young theological student of my own day who was on the point of writing his thesis. He had a card index of his material; it was beautifully arranged with red ink, black ink, tabs, and notches. He was so absorbed in it that days slipped by, and every day there was added improvement. After a while he stopped thinking of his thesis and could think of nothing but the index. The last I heard of it, it was a better index than ever! *That will happen to anybody who lets it!*

And there is no greater peril. Said one acquaintance to another, "I hear the world is coming to an end. What shall we do about it?" Replied the other, "We must fix on a suitable date and have a luncheon!" It is not difficult in our day to mistake machinery for piety, and the management of religious appliances for the signs of a devout mind. It is not difficult to identify bustle with vitality, and to choose motion as if it were proof positive of zeal; in the phrase of Bishop Gore, "seeking refuge from the rigors of thought in opportunities for action." "When a man," writes Kierkegaard, "storms about early and late for the sake of the Good, hurling himself into time as a sick man throws himself down upon his bed, throwing off all consideration for himself as a sick man throws off his clothes, scornful of the world's reward—when such a man makes a place among men, then the masses think what he himself imagines: that he is inspired. And yet he is at the other pole from that, for he is double-minded, and double-mindedness no more resembles inspiration than a tornado the steadiness of the standing wind." One is not always "doing the most business when one seems to be the most busy." There is such a thing as the mechanics of religion, and there are hundreds of preachers who are lost in it. Maurice Maeterlinck tells of an old mansion in Bruges with this motto carved on one of the beams: "Within me there is more." I commend it to you.

We are not, of course, to conclude that the pulpit is the only vantage point from which a preacher may truly and powerfully minister the word of God. There is a proclamation of God's judgments and God's grace which can be made only by the kind of life a man leads. Some of the most zealous of all the servants of Christ and of his church are those beloved ministers in almost every township who have given themselves gallantly not so much to the work of preaching as to the works of mercy and to the service of the whole community in counsel and leadership. They occupy high places in the public regard; unique places, some of them, and rightly. Yet in no instance that has come under my observation would more careful preparation for Sunday have been either impossible or without added influence and effect. It is so distressingly easy to let the emphasis shift from the sermon to the hospital or the town hall, to the other side of the railroad or to international affairs; and to justify that shift, especially if a man feels that he lacks certain gifts as a preacher. To me it is a disastrous shift. I can find no substitute for this thing that we are sent here primarily to do.

Jesus, you will observe, had no illusions on the subject. At the beginning of his ministry in Galilee he could have won tremendous popularity simply by rearranging his time so that there would be less opportunity for preaching, less importance attached to it, and more room, in his case, for the blind and the lame, the lepers and the deaf. Deliberately, in solitude and prayer, he made his choice. Not that any true ministry of mercy was neglected; his love could never have been bound or gagged or kept from running out to needy folk with both hands wide open: but that before even this and under it, the ministry of the Word had all the years priority, the good news imparted to human souls in the sacrament of speech, in fleeting syllables that would not pass away though heaven and earth were gone (Matthew 24:35). He knew what came first. With quiet confidence he turned to those around him. *As ye go*—this was his sober charge—*preach*. (Matthew 10:7) And after him one who had caught his spirit drew a line and cast up the total: *In the presence of God and of Christ Jesus who will judge the living and the dead, in the light of his appearance and his reign, I adjure you to preach the word; keep at it in season and out of season.* (II Timothy 4:1–2) Humanity is still a "wilderness calling for a voice." The only thing in God's economy that can ever take the place of preaching is better preaching. And every man is capable of that. Not of good preaching. Good preaching may be beyond us quite. But better preaching. That is beyond none of us!

And may I say that I do not see how it is possible at all without that other and constant ministry which used to be called "the cure of souls"? *You are*

Gods' Field to Be Planted

writes Paul to the Corinthians (I Corinthians 3:9), *God's house to be built.* I would not even intimate that this more distinctly pastoral office may ever be used as a means to an end. It is, nevertheless, an essential to all preaching that is worthy the name. The day may come—I hope it will—when we shall not be required or expected to be expert in half a dozen different directions. Others with more special training may relieve us of dancing continual attendance on all the enterprises of religious education, social service, and church management; but no one can ever make unnecessary for us that contact with men and women which sometimes goes disrespectfully by the name of "bell-pushing" or "the front-door ministry." There is no other road into the knowledge of human life and human need; and there is no other road down which you may travel half so effectively, if not toward the heart, then toward the crown of your ministry, which is the pressing home of the gospel of Jesus Christ to the individual souls of your people.

I wish you would read that "magnificent exposition of the preachers' task," as A. T. Robertson called it,[12] which Paul has left us in his second letter to the Corinthians (2:12–6:10), and see how it centers just here. *I live for God as the fragrance of Christ breathed alike on those who are being saved and on*

*those who are perishing, to the one a deadly fragrance that*
*makes for death, to the other a vital fragrance that makes for*
*life* (2:15, 16). *Do I need to be commanded by written certifi-*
*cates? You are my certificate yourselves, written on my heart.*
*. . . You are a letter of Christ which I have been employed to*
*inscribe* (3:1, 2, 3). All the great novelists that ever lived, as
James Black has pointed out, the great artists, the great drama-
tists, the great poets, were great by virtue of the fact that they
had in their possession the deep secrets of the life that surged
and eddied about them; secrets that only they learn who live
and love and move joyously where its tides are strongest. *God*
*is our witness that I yearn for you all.* So writes Paul to the
Philippians (1:8). And when as a stranger he must address
himself to those strangers at Rome, *How unceasingly I always*
*mention you in my prayers* (Romans 1:9); closing his letter
with that long list of names—Greeks and Romans and Asiatics,
slaves and free, many of them his friends, every one of them
firmly set in his heart.

You may begin your career with a doctrinaire interest in
theology or in preaching as one of the fine arts. But pray God
you may find yourself, little by little, drawn to human lives and
human hopes and human fears! You may begin with the aloof-
ness of the scholar. But pray God you may continue with a
tenderness, a warmth of affection for all the weary souls of
earth, that will go far to keep you human and to make you
great.

They told me when I went to New York that regular pastoral
visits were neither essential nor particularly desired; and for
a while I believed it. As long as I believed it, I tried it. But since
then I have not only endeavored to make my way in some orderly fashion into as many of the homes of my congregation
as possible, but I have attempted to do it I hope with some in-
creasing emphasis, especially during these days when life is so

tense, on the true aim of all such work: *to set everyone before God*

### Mature in Christ*

And soberly I have come to the conclusion that not only is it unnecessary, but it is a shameful betrayal of my office, to pass the time on such occasions in "idle puerilities" and petty effeminacies devoid of spiritual significance, *gadding about,* as the apostle put it, albeit in another connection, *from one house to another—not merely idle but gossips and busybodies* (I Timothy 5:13, said of young widows). If your life is charged with anything, there are not many times now when it touches another that without strain and without piosity something may not happen in the Kingdom of God. I like to think of that day when Paul's life touched Luke's, up there in Troas; and a gentile physician who it may be had come in to see a sick Jew went out to be an author and a saint. Anybody who is in desperate earnest, as God is, can make of even the most casual exchange not simply a check opposite a name in a book but a highway into eternal life for that other and for his own soul also.

I say for his own soul also because you will find, as I have found, that these people whom you will visit are frequently of far greater service to you than you are to them. I am thinking now of a simple Danish butler who, in the last hours of a long and bitter disease, turned toward me his grateful, patient eyes, with the light in them of the knowledge of the glory of God; and of a woman, nearer to me than that, who sat bound with a grip of iron to her chair, and whose face was still fair and her mouth ever and again full of laughter. These were ministers to me, not I to them. To enter with them hand in hand into the holy places of God's love and peace is to be unspeakably enriched.

* Colossians 1:28.

For my own part, let me say that I have undertaken deliberately through the years, sometimes almost desperately, to multiply the number of these contacts. I have done my best, steadily, to encourage private interviews at the office; not only for those hours of special need which come to all of us, but regularly along the normal way of Christian life, that together as a people and a family of God we may grow in such grace as separately we could not. And I have tried to prepare myself for those interviews as well as I could by some study of psychology and even of the principles of modern psychiatry, though I would hasten to warn all who need warning that we may not regard ourselves as expert in this bewildering field just because we have read Dr. Link's *Return to Religion* or something by Leslie Weatherhead. The chief value of all your preparation at this point may well lie in the ability you acquire to decide what is within your reach and what is not!

Moving still in that same direction, in order to enlarge and supplement the pastoral and individual character of my ministry, I have for twenty years held annually, sometimes at the houses of members, sometimes at the church, a series of group meetings during the course of which it is my privilege to sit down with those who are most intent upon the development and exercise of a true and whole and creative Christian faith. I have discovered with them their difficulties, their hopes, their disappointments, their fears; have spoken to them much more intimately than I can speak in the pulpit; and have learned from them many a time the love and loyalty of quiet lives down unexpected paths.

It is precisely this love and this loyalty which are to be gathered up and given direction in the church's program of personal evangelism. In the last analysis, of course, here is the only program the church has. It is my firm conviction that never in the world will Christianity come into its own until the lay men and lay women of our congregations become once more eager bearers of its gospel, and un-self-conscious witnesses to its power. There never has been any other plan. Certainly none of our attempts to short-cut it has met with any success. There never will be any other plan. I have seen gatherings of ministers and leaders casting about in a panic for some device by which church membership might be augmented. Outstanding clergymen from other cities would be invited, from time to time, to come in and share the secrets of their success. And there is no secret. Jesus himself, at the very start, gave it all away: *As the Father sent me, I am sending you* (John 20:21).

We have got to face it sooner or later. To me it has become increasingly obvious that there is not much room left in the church for people who are content to occupy its pews as disciples only. This living Word of God is nobody's appointed prerogative; and it is nobody's inherited possession: it is everybody's shared and common responsibility. Until we as ministers come to see that ourselves, until we come to strive toward it with a kind of obstinate tenacity, there will simply be no future worth mentioning. Nobody nowadays should have any truck with the idea that what the Germans and the Japanese believe is their business only. It becomes our business with startling suddenness. The notion that a man's religion is a private affair between him and his Maker is what the Archbishop of Canterbury said it was, "astonishingly silly." You and I and these others with us do not wash our hands of the man next door or up the street or at the other end of town in any such casual fashion as that; not in God's world. We do not turn Christianity into a matter of individual choice and complete social indifference,— not with impunity; nor do we lose sight of the fact that when the fires of our religion no longer kindle other fires, its own fires have gone out. There is a penalty which life exacts in the face of all negligence and in contempt of all excuse and argument. The Christianity that no longer propagates itself is no longer Christianity. The faith that has lost its drive has lost its charter. The church that stakes its future on programs is a doomed church.

The preacher, then, even to be a preacher, must be a pastor. From no other source save one, which I shall try in a moment to indicate, can spring that vibrant urgency of spirit which is so utterly indispensable and which in Paul seems to have savored the very passion of God. *I bear branded on my body*
The Owner's Stamp of Jesus*

You can fairly hear him move; it is like the tread of strong feet, down the nights and down the days, down the arches of the years,

> with unhurrying chase,
> And unperturb-ed pace,
> Deliberate speed, majestic instancy.[13]

As I think of the truly great preachers whom I myself have had an opportunity to hear, I realize that this is by far the most thrilling thing about them. They come apparently under a real necessity to be and say "something of such a kind that if men disregard or repudiate it, they will exhaust the patience of God with their generation and life will become a bitter thing."[14] Their words rush out at every listening soul from their own hot and pulsing faith in the message they bear, and from their yearning toward the world of human hopes and human fears which brought them there to bear it. They know the evil that besets me. They never underrate it. They never speak loftily about it, or contemptuously, or sarcastically, as if they themselves were free of the heavy indictment. Not as a judge, with oracular dignity, but as a companion of my way, they come straight from the Companion of theirs; without pretense or

* Galatians 6:17.

wordiness, they report to me what they have found, and share
with me the breath of life.[15]

And I tell you that when no such driving wind blows to fill
a man's sails, when he stands there in his pulpit as if his presence, while expected, were unnecessary, then it is that body and
blood slip out of all the transactions of that place, and there
abides with his people nothing but the uneasy memory of an
hour scarcely more authentic than the starched rhetoric which
tried to fill it. Such an experience Emerson had that snowy day
he went to church and was sorely tempted never to go again.

The snow storm was real [so he wrote]; the preacher merely spectral, and the eye felt the sad contrast in looking at him and then
out of the window behind him, into the beautiful meteor of the
snow. He had no word intimating that he had laughed or wept,
was married or in love, had been commended, or cheated, or cha-
grined. If he had ever lived or acted, we were none the wiser for
it. The capital secret of his profession, namely, to convert life into
truth, he had not learned.[16]

So does the preacher's task enlarge as you draw nearer. There
is no other calling on earth that offers such scope to a man's
powers and makes such demands on his diligence. In no other
is he quite so free to chart his own course. Wherefore in no
other is the lure to idleness more insistent. In no other is the
slippery slope into incompetence more nearly ubiquitous,—to
speak more roundly than anyone should ever speak! And
surely in no other are the penalties for trifling and carelessness
and neglect swifter or more devastating and complete!

Yet for all its reach and freedom as we have tried to look
along it this way and that, we have still not come upon its
greatest dimension. To be a preacher, a man must be a pastor;
to be either, he must be a man whose knowledge of God, far
from being academic, is intimate and authoritative. *I am no
speaker, perhaps,* writes Paul, *but knowledge I do possess* (II
Corinthians 11:6).

### I Know Whom I Have Trusted*

Out of that intimacy alone comes his deepest, truest understanding of the central mysteries of our religion. I hold in memory and in affection a man who had been for thirty years and more an active, loyal, devoted member of the Christian church; until, under bitter circumstances, he lost not only the position he had occupied for a quarter of a century in the educational world but lost with it his faith in those with whom he had been associated. After attempting suicide he tried to make a come-back by way of religion. He went about eagerly listening to the most distinguished ministers of our time, trying to glean something that would be of genuine use to him in his extremity. One of them said in a sermon that we had to verify every truth by our own experience. That stuck. He went home and tried to verify the love of God by his experience. And it would not wash. Another quoted startling instances of answered prayer. He went home and shut his eyes and clenched his hands in an agony of petition; but that would not wash either. Never in his life had it occurred to him, never had it been brought home, that the mysteries of the Christian religion are fundamentally the mysteries of a personal relationship between God and the human soul. He had been fed with efforts to intellectualize what is at bottom the exchange of life with life. He should never have tried submitting any truth to the test of his warped experience, not God's love nor his wife's. He should never have been encouraged to suppose—and he was, at odd times—that there was anything magical about prayer. All that ever was in it, or ever will be, is not what we want; but what is better than what we want —the issues of a great friendship, enabling us when we must, by the knowledge of His will, to bear God's silences!

This love on the throne of the world, this vast efficacy of

* II Timothy 1:12.

prayer,—every one of the central sanctities of the Christian faith finds its truest interpretation in that realm of meeting where the "thou" of God and the "I" of my lonely soul stand solemnly face to face in the mutual give and take of friend with friend. Whatever happens to people, read it that way for them, and it will make sense. They do not want reasons, even when they think they do; they want insights. They do not want anybody with questions. They want somebody with answers; but not facile answers that have never been within a mile of their distress. They want you to tell them what you know; and their faces haunt you in your sleep. Tell them that, and it will go home with them and keep knocking on the door of their heart. Say it stumblingly, say it poorly; but say it, because it is part of you: and some of them, at least, will cry themselves into forgetfulness that night. They want somebody who does not have to run like a distant page through long and winding corridors, whispering what someone has told him, having heard it from someone else, who in turn had got it from another, to one of whose acquaintances the King had spoken and expressed His sovereign will. You and I are here not to listen curiously at the threshold of other lives for some report that will fit our fancy; we are here ourselves to enter into that intimate association from which alone a man can come and on the ground of his own discovery give voice to the Word that is not his own. *Thus saith the Lord.*

I wonder at times if anything more is needed to catch the wistful stare of men and women in our generation; anything but this sure sound, as if one had been off on a journey and returned with news. That way you will never have to cover up uncertainties with intolerance or balance with a bigoted and dogmatic front your dark and hidden insecurities. Such narrow moods of the soul come of nothing but of trying to double the emphasis for lack of any competence in the proof. Conviction that is strong and deep it not argumentative; it is not merely intellectual or philosophical or academic. It is what love is in Paul's catalogue of shining dignities: It *suffereth long and is kind*. It *envieth not*. It *vaunteth not itself, is not puffed up, doth not behave itself unseemly, seeketh not* its *own, is not easily provoked, thinketh no evil* (I Corinthians 13, A.V.). It is a moral state that comes not of theory but of experiment; not of being expert in biblical criticism but of being expert in that long pilgrimage toward the City of God which the Bible records; not of familiarity with any doctrine, or with the philosophies of any bygone age, but of the knowledge of One Who is Himself the Truth, to Whom all stammering philosophies must come at last to hold out their hands or perish. It is something that comes of the God we preach and out of the anguish of soul which He alone knows how to stir and how to still.

What else is there on the threshold of a changing world, where the wealth and poverty of all our yesterdays move in upon the promise or the threat of tomorrow,—what else that can lift its head and lead men toward the peace and the power of a still and mighty Presence?

*Of what existed from the very beginning, of what we heard, of what we saw, of what we witnessed and touched with our own hands, . . . we bring you word, . . . so that you may share our fellowship; and our fellowship is with the Father and with his Son Jesus Christ* (I John 1:1-3).

*I too believe and so I speak* (II Corinthians 4:13).

**⊷ॐ ৡৡ**

This noble ensample to his sheep he yaf,
That first he wroghte, and afterward he taughte.

*The Canterbury Tales,* Prologue

✓✓✓✓✓✓✓✓✓✓✓✓✓✓✓✓✓✓✓✓✓✓✓✓✓✓✓✓✓✓✓✓✓✓✓✓✓✓✓✓✓✓✓✓✓✓

# Chapter 2

## LIKE A MAN OF GOD*

✓✓✓✓✓✓✓✓✓✓✓✓✓✓✓✓✓✓✓✓✓✓✓✓✓✓✓✓✓✓✓✓✓✓✓✓✓✓✓✓✓✓✓✓✓✓

We have seen thus far that the preacher's task makes certain minimum demands upon him in these three different relations: in the pulpit, as a pastor among his people, and as a witness to the everlasting Yea and Amen of God in his own soul. But behind his duties and his privileges, back of them all in every relation, is the decisive fact of his own personality. That is central and conclusive. At the heart of his pastoral ministrations, in the solemn loneliness of those hours when he lifts his face to the Eternal, lending his lips to that Other Will and to "the things most surely believed," always in the midst, he stands, himself a man! And from the manner of man he is shall ever be drawn the true quality and reach of his power. Suppose we try to see him, quite simply and directly, back of his work.

* II Corinthians 2:17.

More than anything else, it seems to me, he must be a man "possessed." With what urgency Paul writes to the people of Corinth:

### You Are Not Your Own*

He is sure that this one conviction, if it runs deep enough, will give a man's whole life direction, as indeed it will. *What do you possess,* he wants to know, *that has not been given you? And if it was given you, why do you boast as if it had been gained, not given?* (I Corinthians 4:7) I sometimes wonder how we ever got the idea that we own anything. Certainly we are living in a world that does not belong to us. We do not own our talents. Whatever the capacity we have, all of it came straight out of the blue; and we have no sure and lasting tenure on any of it. George Eliot used to say that nothing she had ever written was hers, really; it was handed to her. She just had to reach out and take it. An artist recently told me the same thing in almost the same words. One hardly needs to belabor the point. I do not know what it is that we own. Maybe some day we shall quit acting like proprietors and start behaving like guests.

There is this matter of health, for instance, and the way so many of us think we have it; then we impose on it. We are not all equally endowed at this point, or indeed at any other. Here and there are near-invalids occupying Christian pulpits with more effect than a baker's dozen of near-athletes like some of us. But we do have in common the responsibility of maintaining as best we can such physical and mental well-being as is ours by nature or cultivation. You will have to find out for yourself, preferably on the advice of a capable physician, what that responsibility involves for you. It may mean diet, as it did for me; it may mean stated periods in the open air; it may mean any one of a score of disciplines. My word to you is that you

* I Corinthians 6:20.

regard and treat this aspect of your ministry as fundamental. *The training of the body* may be *of small service,* as Paul says, when you compare it with training *for the religious life* (I Timothy 4:8); but squanderers of health are quite as culpable as any other squanderers and profligates. They will answer for it. The plain fact is that you cannot serve God as you might with an instrument that you have abused; whether from ignorance or with full knowledge, whether by harmful habits or by careless inattention makes no difference. And Life and God will some day render their account and want to know why. They rendered an account to me a few years ago in the guise of a strained larynx, for which there was to pay six months of anything but golden silence. Today I have both eyes open a little wider than either was before to the limitations which lie upon the strongest of us and, when snubbed, even though unwittingly, turn our course into no more than a fool's race against inexorable and swift reality!

One thing is certain: it is rarely if ever the burden of work we have to fear. The preachers who are always indulging in self-pity on that score are a private nuisance to themselves and a public nuisance to the Kingdom of God. Not excess of work, but wrong methods; lack of balance; moral, mental, or spiritual maladjustment. Upon them follow blue Mondays, irritable Tuesdays, nervous Wednesdays, and the whole Pandora's box of clamant ills to which our ministerial flesh seems peculiarly heir, and from which, be it said, we might well have been delivered by a reasonable watchfulness, by the due proportion of daily exercise and rest, by the pursuit and relaxation of some hobby, and—shall we add—by the proper and consistent use of summer vacations for the building up not alone of physical but also of cultural reserves.

Other things being equal a man, though a clergyman, can be on the whole, for many a long year of active service, vigorous and well, if he will only insist upon being moderately intelligent, and make it his business to know himself and to deal with himself wisely in that knowledge. Health in a very real sense is a part of the Christian gospel, as it is often the definitive measure of a minister's usefulness.

But I would speak more particularly now of that farther, deeper realm, where character is born. Let him here above all things else take

### A Sane View of Himself*

I want to be just as prosaic at this point, just as plebeian and factual, just as little idealistic and visionary, as I can. No one would go so far as to say that the minister should be a bad man; but I will unhesitatingly go far enough to cry aloud with all my might against expecting of him more saintliness than is human! At his ordination he promises "to adorn the doctrine of our Saviour by a holy life and conversation." But I protest his canonization by the people who adore him. He is a poor, benighted sinner like the rest, "standing in the need of prayer." He is in the battle and not above it. He is subject to temptation, and he is subject to defeat in fighting it. If he does not know that to begin with, he will soon stumble on it; and he ought not to keep the knowledge from his congregation or from his wife and children! He is not necessarily a spiritual giant, mighty in all the affairs of the soul; and God forbid that he should pose as one of such stature. Entering the ministry is no guarantee that the wrestling will go more smoothly with you, against principalities, against powers, against the rulers of the darkness of this world (Ephesians 6:12 A.V.). When you smack into that knowledge for yourself some day, do not be discouraged. A minister is a man; let him remember that he is and act as a man. Surely there are things he will do that other men would not even think of doing; and

* Romans 12:3.

there are things which others do that he will not. But he will
take to himself no unction on that account, as if he alone had
succeeded in putting a pinch of salt on "the tails of the seven
deadly virtues!"

This of course is the weak spot in the armor of all legalists
in religion. Paul writes of it in the second chapter of Colossians,
verses 20–23: *Why submit to*

Rules and Regulations

*like "Hands off this!"*
*"Taste not that!" "Touch not this!"—referring to things that*
*perish by being used? These rules are determined by human*
*precepts and tenets; they get the name of "wisdom" with their*
*self-imposed devotions, with their fasting, with their rigorous*
*discipline of the body, but they are of no value, they simply*
*pamper the flesh!*

True character is not built by obedience to moral precept,
however ascetic and strict. That holds for the layman and it
holds for the priest. Such outward purity as some folk achieve
on one side of their lives, ministers among them, is too often
matched by an impurity on some other side not so manifest,
perhaps by acidity of disposition, by self-consciousness, by spiritual pride, by jealousy, by a cruel and sadistic temper.[1] There
are those who try to make up for secret immoralities of thought
and practice by the most meticulous habits of physical cleanliness! There are others who find in a sort of hyperorthodoxy an
escape from the relentless ethical demands of this troublesome
Christ. Whatever else the mind is, it is a highly formidable
piece of compensating machinery. All moralists in the pulpit
and out of it should make a diligent note of that. You would be
amazed to know what latitude "good" people allow themselves
off-stage.

Such a puritanical approach to religion, such prim and
priggish behavior, never achieves even at best much more than

a policing of the riotous, imprisoned forces within. And may heaven guard the public when the police cordon breaks! Herman Melville in *Typee* tells of a ten-day festival held once in Hawaii, at the beginning of the nineteenth century, to celebrate the restoration of the native monarchy. The Connecticut blue laws which had been in force under the watchful eyes of the missionaries were revoked and

... the natives almost to a man plunged voluntarily into every species of wickedness, plainly showing by their utter disregard of all decency that though they had been schooled into a seeming submission to a new order of things, they were in reality as depraved and vicious as ever.

It is the constant peril of that Old-Testament view of life which has had such an amazing rebirth in the Christian church of our time and which so rarely seems able to turn by way of love into Christianity. The true relation between morality .and religion has been strikingly suggested by Schleiermacher in a metaphor drawn from music:

A man's special calling is the melody of his life, and it remains a simple, meager series of notes unless religion, with its endlessly rich variety, accompany it with all notes, and raise the simple song to a full-voiced, glorious harmony.[2]

And so I suggest that in attempting to construct for ourselves a sort of matter-of-fact working model of the man behind the preacher's task, we begin not with any idea of ministerial behavior, that *form of godliness* which may all too often be without its power (II Timothy 3:5, A.V.), but with a minister's first obligation; namely, before being anything else, to be himself—himself at his best in Christ—but still himself. If preaching is the mediation of divine truth through personality—and perhaps with all definitions lame we may accept this as being not more lame than the rest—then the one thing you have to contribute toward the transaction is yourself. The human heart is not new, the need is not new, the truth is not new, the method is not new. You are new. You are a bit of God's unrepeated handiwork; and what he means to accomplish by you, he must accomplish through you. It would be too bad, then, if you should be found a counterfeit presentment of someone else, an imitation in matter or manner of the great or the near-great.

No famous preacher ever lived without having his style and even the tones of his voice borrowed, without interest, be it said, by whole generations of theological students. Much of this sincerest of all flattery is no doubt unconscious; but it is none the less objectionable. And I never have been able to understand how anybody's wife or friends would or could let him get away with it. They ought to sandpaper him down to the quick! Deliberate imitation of the masters in strategy and approach may be, in fact, I believe it is, a most helpful discipline. In his early days, and for many years after, Dr. Jowett used to practice the analysis of texts and the outlining of sermons in the mood now of Spurgeon, now of Dale, now of Bushnell, or Maclaren, or Whyte. But habitually to assume, even though unintentionally, the pose of another, to take on his accents, to pattern after his mind, sometimes after even his gestures—this is to be no one truly, with no claim upon anybody's respect.

To be only yourself six days in the week and on the seventh to be no other, whether in reading the service or in preaching the sermon, may not be very thrilling; but it is the only hope there is for you. Never belittle that self or despise it; never disown it or betray it. You have nothing else but you. Give it reverence and give it freedom. To cut through all artificialities of bearing, to put off all the pompous habits of a false dignity, to hang somewhere on a hook all the seeming which is so far other than being, and to let that essential you, redeemed and enabled in the love and fellowship of Jesus Christ, do its proper work in the world—that is to turn loose something God has never tried before; and He will never try it again: make what you please of that!

Certainly this is not to say that in the effort to be ourselves we are to become long-haired individualists. Like everybody else we have to keep correcting our course and veering away from extremes: on the one hand, from the rubbing out in this way or that of all the distinctive qualities which make us what we are; and on the other, from that exaggeration of angularities and prejudices, tastes and distastes, which render it so difficult for some of us to do anything co-operatively with the rest of us. It is *our* advice that must be borne aloft like a torch in the council room. It is *our* will that must triumph. Or you will find us sooner or later withdrawing from your project, albeit regretfully, and wholly for conscience's sake. To have a mind of your own is to be another chance for the Kingdom in the hands of God; to have no mind but your own is to be no more than the ghost of that chance forever.

Then, surely, the minister must be a man versed
In Prayer and Supplication*

I have already spoken of a friend who through bleak days and weeks and months sought from pulpits and from ministers in the privacy of their studies some way out for his harassed soul. He has told me that few if any ever suggested that they kneel down together and pray God. To this day he wonders if there is anything in prayer, if clergymen themselves believe in it.

"I cried out in the darkness for help," so he wrote, "but the mountains of memory and need only echoed my cries. Frustrated, disillusioned, bewildered, I traveled a vicious circle, always returning to the question: What have I a right to expect through prayer? And because there was no answer close at

* Philippians 4:6.

hand, I wondered: Do preachers pray? Must they face disaster and death, besieged in a foxhole, before they can pray alone with a layman?"

I have still the questionnaire he sent out. Perhaps the results of it would interest you. From one hundred sixty-five ministers approached he received fifty-four replies. Thirty-nine per cent admitted "spells of irregularity," six per cent seldom engaged in private devotions, and nine per cent did not intend to establish any "system." Thirty-nine per cent were hesitant to initiate prayer alone with an intelligent, well-balanced layman. Forty-six per cent made no organized effort in the education and training of adults with regard to the habit and practice of prayer.

"Have the brilliant liberals of the church," my friend went on, "the intelligentsia, a new revelation of God which they hesitate to disclose for fear that the laity cannot bear the truth? Perhaps laymen do not need to pray except vicariously, en masse, Sundays, or when about to die. Perhaps modernity has outmoded prayer. Perhaps the clergy are convinced they can make the world Christian by preaching, by education and reason, rather than by faith. Perhaps man must feed his soul on science. Perhaps the Christian religion is merely a code of ethics. Perhaps the world can be saved by men who organize to put over a perfect social system. Perhaps man must rely on himself alone, support himself unaided, lift himself by his own bootstraps. If prayer is vital, if it really does work, why doesn't he hear more from the pulpit about how to relate it to everyday living? Why isn't he taught by the church what he has a right to expect through prayer?"

There is nothing that lies nearer the center of the Christian ministry than this. Our poverties here cannot long be concealed. The day comes when they are shouted from the housetops. Our private evasions become our public futilities. Our secret barrenness of soul is made the open shame of all our ways. Again I want to be honest, pretending nothing. I want to say what is true. There are experiences of which some men write that are quite beyond me. Dr. Andrew Bonar, in his diary, tells of whole days given over to prayer, of nights spent in confession and intercession. It may be my own sin that I am confessing when I say that such testimony as that leaves me thoroughly dazed and very definitely on the outside of a locked door. As far as I am concerned, even an hour spent in prayer, one-third of Luther's habitual practice, would be, I am afraid, unless you are very generous in your definition of praying, the next thing to an utter impossibility. And I am bold enough to believe that I am not alone in my embarrassment.

But let me hurry to add that for me and my kind prayer need be none the less real. It must certainly have its sacred periods and its unremitting disciplines, lest the spirit of it be lost. It is not a mere "talking with God, commonplace and trivial." Nor is it "something entirely spontaneous, inward, informal, and unregularized," the "effort to produce a vaguely devotional mood." In that fascinating little volume by C. S. Lewis, *The Screwtape Letters*, this is precisely the kind of prayer the devil wants: not one who prays with "moving lips and bended knees," but one who like Coleridge merely "composes his spirit to love" and indulges in "a sense of supplication." Praying, wrote Alexander Whyte, is colossal work. It is the nakedness of a soul intent before God—heart and mind and will, answering deep unto deep.

Yet for all that I submit that among the dearest of all its ministries may well be for you as for me those fleeting moments of known companionship which come in the way of a day's duty, whispered confidences, when the angel, so to speak, of a man's own presence, of its six great wings, with twain would cover its face, and with twain would cover its feet, while with twain it would fly. To open at each appointed time the quiet door of some holy place; to stand there before God with all this confused business of living spread out at His feet; to see it as He sees it; and then to shoulder it again in the light of His countenance, not really having known what we should pray for as we ought, but knowing even as we despair of ourselves that *the Spirit pleads for us with sighs that are beyond words* (Romans 8:26): that is to pray. But to sit in the quiet of your own study, before your mind's eye the people you serve, the things that hurt them and drive some of them away to nurse their hurt in private, the things that perplex them and defeat them, the things that light up their faces with love and hope and joy, —to sit there with all that before you, writing the prayer in which you mean to lead them on Sunday straight to the Throne of God: this, too, is to pray. And why not write that prayer? Before ever you attempt to stand with them on the threshold of eternity and presume there to put into words their deepest needs and yearnings! Why not write it? Then to climb the steps of a pulpit, conscious of the soft tread of other feet, of the sound of Another's voice, and the friendly pressure of His hand! That, too, is to pray. Or to be called some noon from the shadow of your own brooding and be sent hurrying to the bedside of a little child; to feel on your brow as you go the coolness of God, like the touch of a father, smoothing away every vestige of your anxiety with this simple, kindly thing he has given you to do for him; to come home in the evening, with the red flame of a dying day on His altar in the west, and to be glad still in One Who all the days shall bless thee and keep thee and cause His face to shine upon thee: it is prayer. And only God Himself, I think, knows how poor life is without it.

With whatever aids to private devotion may best suit your purpose—George Buttrick in his really great book on *Prayer* lists many of them—make your own brave and steady excursions into that fabled country. *Attend to your prayers* (Colossians 4:2). Nor ever be content, as though you had explored its farthest horizons. The difficulties we have with it, as Daniel Jenkins of Birmingham University in England points out, are not what we think they are: how to find time for it, how to square it with scientific interpretations of the universe. The difficulties we have with it come of allowing ourselves to be "strapped in the prison house" of our own lives.[3] So do we "console ourselves with experience," or "tune in on the infinite," the most unrewarding, the most futile practice in all the world; or we pour forth freely the longings of our hearts, "forgetting that it is precisely the heart which the prophet describes as *deceitful above all things, and desperately wicked*." (Jeremiah 17:9, A.V.)

Rather must we come as those who by their prayer would blaze a trail into this wide and virgin land, on the shores of which, barely on its shores, despairing of themselves wondering multitudes have stood, waiting only upon God, if He will condescend to hear; while back in the hills, his garments fluttering like the great white plume of Navarre, moves ever one haunting, beckoning Figure, calling to us over his shoulder, *Ask and the gift will be yours, seek and you will find, knock and the door will open to you; for everyone who asks receives, the seeker finds, the door is opened to anyone who knocks* (Matthew 7:7, 8; Luke 11:9, 10). We watch him out of sight toward the mountains and the dawn: and when he comes again we too, with those others of old, knowing the secret of His power, shall look up into his face and say still, "Lord, teach us to pray!"

But as the true minister is a man of prayer, so also must he be a man who lives

By Faith in the Son of God*

Which, among
other things, comes to this: that in his reckoning and to his certain knowledge all he can say or do multiplies itself straightway by the Infinite. Whatever the present, in this so often desperate world, he gives himself to the future and to the task of
transforming as much of human life each day as he can reach.
And you will not oppress his spirit; for he is in this venture
with Another. He is not building for ultimate ruin. Even his
tears, if you please, and broken hopes, are part of the order being hewn out of chaos, part of the music which God will fashion out of sound. His is a faith which like Joan of Arc's has its
voices; and they keep crying, *The kingdoms of this world are
become the kingdoms of our Lord, and of his Christ* (Revela-
tions 11:15, A.V.).

He is not inclined therefore to estimate the importance of a
service by the attendance. The Book of Numbers is not to him
the most highly esteemed and best thumbed book in the Bible.
He moves with quietness and with poise instead of in that love
of the moment which "falsifies eternity." He believes that the
Word he utters is not his, but of God Who sent him. He is not
therefore busy in his own mind setting limits to it, doubting its
power, asking questions about its effectiveness. The might
*exerted in raising Christ from the dead* (Ephesians 1:20) dwells
in it. He understands that something always happens when that
Word is spoken in sincerity and truth. He may know nothing
of those happenings. Many a soul will steal into a pew and steal
out of it with never a syllable, not even a glance to indicate that
the winter now is past, and "the time of the singing of birds" is
come. "No news of their spring," writes Dr. Jowett, "gets into
his journal." But there it is.

When others approve of him, he will not be hypocrite enough

* Galatians 2:20.

to say even to himself that their approval is distasteful to him—
though the devil in most cases will have told him how good
he was before anybody else has said a word.[4] But he will not
strive for that approval, before God he will not. And if it comes,
deep down somewhere inside, deeper than any voice, will be
a quiet song of praise to Him of Whom and through Whom
and to Whom are all things. Preferment, jealousy of those more
fortunate than he, issuing in cheap criticism, in rivalry and resentments,—these will be to him a dread profanity making the
whole round of life unclean.

Nor will he hold back because he thinks some task too great;
or rush by it with contempt because he thinks it is too small.
I got a letter not long ago from one who told me the true
story of a lonely girl and a "popular" minister. Their lives almost touched one evening, for just a moment. "She was in desperate trouble," my friend wrote; "I don't know what, but I can
guess. She went to see him, went to his home, to talk to him.
He was so well-known thereabouts that even she knew him. But
he was at dinner with his guests. She waited for some time; but
at last he sent back the maid to say that he could not see her;
she should come the next day to his office. That night she went
out and tried to kill herself. A physician just happened to be
on the spot. Fortunately he was not dining, though even if he
had been he could not have refused her need. He had to work
hard and fast, but he pulled her through. I do not know whether
he might not better have let her die. I do not know what became of her. But if she is living today, what do you suppose she
thinks of Jesus Christ and the man who stood that night in his
stead, dining at home with his guests?" Of course, we here
could urge those extenuating circumstances which every minister, I suppose, might cite; but there was really nothing much
to be said. And at such times I have found it wisest not to say
much. To turn our back on even the passing stranger is to

betray first and foremost, it seems to me, our faith in God. With Him about, and that lone girl, who knows? A continent might have been knocking at the door, or a century. Who would dare then to sit still?

And that brings us on. The true minister, because he has faith in God, will have faith, too, in people. You will recall what is perhaps one of the tenderest things in the whole range of Pauline literature: the way the apostle recovered his confidence and his pride in the church at Corinth in spite of the bitter and painful controversy which had raged between them. He writes of it with surpassing kindliness (II Corinthians 7:3–16); but never is there any doubt of the source from which he drew. He had set that down at the start:

Faithful Is the God Who Called You

*to this fellow-ship with His Son Jesus Christ our Lord* (I Corinthians 1:9). It is the quiet look he takes before plunging into the main business of his letter. The gospel he has preached has already begun to bear its fruit. There have been signs of Christ's presence in Corinth. Many lives have been enriched. To some of them the Spirit has given utterance, ecstatic now and then, and in need of control; yet there it was. And this apostle is the last man on earth to close his eyes to it. Much in the present calls for rebuke, and item by item he will go into it. Meanwhile, the past, and God, and this Word for the future. *Faithful is the God who called you.*

I suppose there are times in the experience of every man among us when we are ready to throw up our hands at all humanity's miserable little ways; hours when the temptation to turn cynical is almost irresistible. We begin to feel as Byron felt:

. . . in the crowd
They could not deem me one of such; I stood

Among them, but not of them; in a shroud
Of thoughts that were not their thoughts . . .

Or perhaps as that medieval preacher must have felt, who
wanted to tell his listeners how necessary it was for them to co-
operate with the clergy, and so chose as his text Job 1:14: *The
oxen were plowing, the asses were grazing beside them.* I myself, when I was younger, knew a reverend gentleman who on
his way back to his parish one day from a week of conference
told me that he was heading again for his purgatory!

Then, with us as with Paul, down in the last recesses of being, where the tide of despair must meet something that can
fling it back, there in that last solitude is this: A God Who
keeps faith. An everlasting Yea and Amen about living, and
One Who will stand by it. That is why Jesus was never cynical.
It was his peculiar glory, I have often thought, that for all his
knowing what was in man, not once were his lips curled; not
even on the cross they made for him, with the curses they kept
shouting, and the crude jests that were their last will and testament. Because back of everything, like all the hosts of heaven
moving, was the sound of the Eternal keeping His deathless
watch! *Father, I trust my spirit to thy hands* (Luke 23:46). If
that is how it is, we can afford to be patient, no matter what
happens! We cannot afford to be anything else.

The story is recorded[5] that there was once in Germany a
kindly teacher who dreamed great dreams, and who upon entering the schoolroom would ever doff his hat with reverence
and honor to salute the class in the name of the high and unknown future. And the odd thing was,—or was it the natural
thing? I hardly know!—that on one of those benches sat a boy
whose name was Martin Luther.

When you look into the faces of your congregation, leave
your disappointments at home, and turn your imagination loose
in this amazing world. Speak to their other and better selves.

They have burdens to carry and difficulties to overcome that they have never confided to you. If you knew them as God knows them, or even as they know themselves: what they hope and fear; what they have allowed life to do to them; how they have been hemmed in and driven off in a corner; how lonely they are inside,—maybe you would feel toward them more as God feels. You might even stand in awe of them for all there is about them that is incalculably great.

If you knew, instead of despising them, you might plead for them as Moses pled: *Yet, wilt thou not forgive their sin? If thou wilt not, then pray blot me out of thy list of the living!* (Exodus 33:32)

Galsworthy once remarked, "I think the greatest thing in the world is to believe in people." This much is certain: by no other road shall we ever lure them toward the heights for which they were made.

Faith in God and faith in people! You see at once what this will mean by way of courage. Paul puts it very bluntly to the Philippians (1:28):

Never Be Scared for a Second

The Kingdom of God is not built out of any toadying to the influential, to the wealthy, or to the learned. It is built of that loyalty to the truth as it is in Jesus Christ which keeps a man gentle but very firm; sends him back again and again to start over whenever it is necessary; holds his face in these troubled days toward the dawn of peace and justice in all the earth—steadily, come weal or woe. There may be suffering ahead. Trouble with your own congregation, perhaps—who knows? If you mean to go about with the truth naked in your hands, while you would never deliberately stir up trouble, there is no guarantee that you will not run into it. Rather is Christ's guarantee quite the opposite: *The time is coming,* he said to that little band of his, *when anyone who kills you will imagine he is performing a service to God* (John 16:2). And I am not sure things have changed a great deal. Whoever plans to throw his weight into the scales against war, and on the side of the outcast, the underprivileged and the poor, the share-cropper, the Negro, the Jew, will likely have no "primrose path of dalliance" to tread these next few years. But then, it is always gallantry God wants, and not just a kind of limp amiability that knows how to wear soft clothing and prefers kings' houses. It is going to take courage for you to go the way of love when the world is still, after two thousand years, hating its lovers and crowning them with thorns. It is going to take courage for you to be kind when the world is always quick to take advantage of kindness. It is going to take courage to be a sort of savior when saviors never do fit anywhere but on a cross. It is going to take courage to suffer. What is harder, it will take courage to wait.

And to do it withal cheerfully, never rolling your eyes about and "looking dreadful" in the effort to be impressive; never talking of religion, as Adam Philip has phrased it, in your "poorly voice," as if in one way or another it had made you sick. Writes the apostle (II Corinthians 4:1): *As I hold this ministry by God's mercy to me*

I Never Lose Heart

*in it.* The dull glance and the anxious, worried brow are not just the best advertisement the Christian faith could have, whether in the chancel or out of it. There is such a thing as not having enough religion to enjoy it. The good news is betrayed by dark faces. Marcus Dodds in his diary[6] tells us how bitterly it went with him:

No day passes without strong temptation to give up, on the ground that I am not fitted for pastoral work; writing sermons is often the hardest labor, visiting is terrible. I often stand before a door unable to ring or knock—sometimes I have gone away without entering.

A lowness of spirit that it costs me a great deal to throw off is the consequence of this, and a real doubt whether it would not be better for myself and all whom it may concern that I should at once look for some work that I could overtake.

But Marcus Dodds did not find it necessary to settle down in such moods and dwell there. Listen to him writing on the seventeenth chapter of Genesis:

Faith is not a blind and careless assent to matters of indifference; faith is not a state of mental suspense with a hope that things may turn out to be as the Bible says. Faith is the firm persuasion that these things are so. And he who at once knows the magnitude of these things and believes that they are so must be filled with a joy that makes him independent of the world, with an enthusiasm which must seem to the world like insanity.[7]

It is ever the man who has God in his mind, as deep as his heart, that clambers out of the slough of despond "farthest from his own house, and next to the wicket gate," on his way to a city which hath foundations.

Only the road, and the dawn, the sun, and the wind, and the rain,
And the watch-fire under the stars, and sleep, and the road again.
We travel the dusty road, till the light of the day is dim,
And the sunset shows us spires away on the world's rim.[8]

True gallantry and true gaiety somehow belong together. They march continually hand in hand, exulting in "the precipitousness of life," and loving "the bright face of danger." It was Glover, I believe, who said of the early Christians that they were absurdly happy and always getting into trouble! What else could ever be the upshot of a faith which, instead of being a theory is a harnessed fact?

But there is another cardinal quality that has to be set down if we mean to make the rounds of them. Paul dwells on it in I Corinthians (9:19-22): *Free as I am from all, I have made myself the slave of all, to win over as many as I could. To Jews*

*I have become like a Jew, to win over Jews; to those under
the Law I have become as one of themselves—though I am not
under the Law myself—to win over those under the Law; to
those outside the Law I have become like one of themselves—
though I am under Christ's law, not outside God's Law—to
win over those outside the Law; to the weak I have become as
weak myself, to win over the weak, I have become*

To All Men All Things

*to save some by all*

*and every means.*

I suppose we might call it a kind of moral sensibility, an
awareness to situations, to people, to common human needs, of
which every man has his own: whatever is not callous or crude
or unresponsive or vulgar, blundering along in every place alike
with its clumsy hands and its loud footfall. The minister, in
short, must be a man of feeling. Nor is this simply a matter of
native equipment, of which you can say that you are either possessed of it or you are not, and there is an end. It is a matter
that has to do more with deliberate self-discipline than with
all the occult influences of heredity and environment. We can
every one of us go to school to the fine arts of living.

We can learn, among other things, a certain sensitiveness toward beauty. Lack of appreciation more often than not is little
other than the reflection of complacent indifference. We are
not indifferent to music, to sunsets, to poetry, to El Greco and
van Gogh, because we do not like them; we do not like them
because we are indifferent to them and cannot take the trouble
to be anything else. It is said of Charlotte Brontë that at school
her classmates were amused to see her hold up before her short-
sighted eyes sometimes for hours a common woodcut, scrutiniz-
ing it with the utmost attention; but afterwards she would say
wonderful things about it. And when she got a chance to go
off she did not head for Regent Street where richer girls

spent their time shopping, but for the National Galleries and straight for the best things there. She had educated herself with a woodcut. That man's response was not all foolishness who, when asked if he could play the violin, said he had never tried and therefore could not tell. Nobody knows what powers of appreciation lie dormant within him, nor will he know until he has held himself steadily and long in the presence of some glory that has haunted the human soul.

So also can one either lose or learn a sensitiveness to other men's sorrows. Back in the Old Testament, among the Jews carried captive from Jerusalem to Babylon was a priest, Ezekiel by name, who there before the face of his fellow-exiles in a distant land was to utter the judgments of God; but not until he could see eye to eye as they saw, sitting where they sat, yonder at Tel-a-bib by the banks of the Kebar, in like condition with the poorest, on the sand-heap, surrounded with the debris of many floods, looking down upon the river. And it came to pass that at the end of the seven days the Word of the Lord came unto him (Ezekiel 3:15, 16). Forbearance and yearning and friendship had stalked over and sat down at the center of another's condition, to deal wisely and lovingly with what it found there. And that is no auxiliary grace.

It is the one quality of all others without which nobody's role can ever be played out triumphantly to the end. Lives that go around centered in themselves take hurt at every slight, at every angry word, cherishing their dislikes, their animosities, their antipathies, and their wrongs; lives that are conscious of being set here to lift life and reclaim it know very well that every hurt is an opportunity, every slight a wide-open door. They will come through the hurt and the slight with a love that will heal. Wound them, and they will not go off in a corner and brood. They will get over into your place, ferret out the need that made you wound them, and give themselves to that. *Get thee unto the*

*children of thy people and speak. Then I came to them of the*
*captivity, and I sat where they sat, and remained there seven*
*days.* (A.V.) It is the secret of the Incarnation, which itself is
the ancient pledge of a heart in this world that forever understands. And one can either lose that secret or learn it.

Of Gustave Frenssen, who labored so devotedly during the
last war among humble village folk, when as now the human
race stood bespattered with brothers' blood on a vast barren
plain, feeling that it had been following the wrong road; be-
wailing the fact, yet in distress and doubt not knowing which
road to take,—of him it is written:

His every sermon glows with sympathy. He feels for us. He is
amazed that men can be so cruel as to wrong each other. Though
he knows well the havoc wrought by nature, though as a child he
had seen the lightning strike a great farmhouse and set its barns
and stables on fire, though he had often heard how in former times
the devouring seas engulfed the land, yet he is not distressed at
this. He does not pretend to understand the workings of that mysterious power which rules the world of nature. But that men should
hate each other, should envy each other, should wound each other—
this seems to him a dreadful thing. We were meant to be happy, we
might be happy, and we refuse to be happy. This it is which stirs
him to the very depths. This is the motif of his every novel, this
the basis of almost every sermon which he preached. On well nigh
every page one meets the word "happiness," the happiness that
might be and that ought to be; and side by side with it the grim
reality, man, in spite of all the preaching of all the churches, still
weary and heavy-laden, still wretched, careworn, sad. This it is
that distresses him beyond measure. No one can read his sermons
without feeling that he is in the presence of a personal friend who
is deeply grieved at the care and sorrow, the sin and shame, with
which his happiness is marred.[9]

Some day surely your own scars will teach you, the scars
that have come of living. *The world's pain ends in death;* but
there is, as well of body as of soul,

## The Pain God Is Allowed to Guide*

Without the healing compassion that is born of it your sermon will lie a cripple at the beautiful gate of the temple. Thornton Wilder in one of his three-minute plays, *The Angel That Troubled the Waters,* tells of a man who stood on a day by the pool of Bethesda, praying in fierce agony that God would touch his tortured soul into health. But the angel, coming, whispered in his ear saying, "Stand back; healing is not for you. Without your wound where would your power be? It is your very remorse that makes your low voice tremble into the hearts of men. Not the angels themselves in Heaven can persuade the wretched and blundering children of earth as can one human being broken on the wheels of living. In love's service only the wounded soldiers can serve." And in that moment the angel stepped down into the waters and troubled them. As the lone sufferer drew back, a lame old neighbor, smiling his thanks, made his painful way into the pool and was healed. Joyously, with a song on his lips, he approached the other, still standing there like a statue of grief, thinking of the things which might have been. "Perhaps," said he, "it will be your turn next! But meanwhile come with me to my house. My son is lost in dark thoughts. I do not understand him. Only you have ever lifted his mood. And my daughter, since her child has died, sits in the shadow. She will not listen to us. Come with me but an hour!" *I would make up the full sum of all that Christ has to suffer in my person* (Colossians 1:24).

It is this true and deep compassion, springing from your own encounter with life, this *favor of suffering* (Philippians 1:29), worn like the king's sackcloth under your royal robes, within upon your flesh (II Kings 6:30), that will at last keep you merciful and tender, *with insight, patience, kindness, the holy*

* II Corinthians 7:10.

*Spirit, unaffected love, true words, the power of God* (II Corinthians 6:6, 7).
*Blessed be the God and Father of our Lord Jesus Christ . . .*
The God of All Comfort

*who comforts me in all my distress, so that I am able to comfort people who are in any distress by the comfort with which I myself am comforted by God* (II Corinthians 1:3, 4). "Be kind," Ian Maclaren used to say; "be kind: every man you meet is fighting a hard battle." Nothing else can guard you from that unconscious severity which comes so often of inexperience and makes many a preacher's sermons seem about as inviting as a mailed fist. Listen to this sample which was sent me:

There is one thing the grace of God cannot do for sinful men. Grace cannot give them the history they never lived! The robber who died beside Jesus is today fellowshipping with apostles, prophets, martyrs, confessors; but they have one thing he has not, and can never have. They have the beauty of their accumulated history, their loyalties, their sacrifices, their heroisms. His history is barren, save for its one last magnificent choice. His works had all to be burned. He went out into eternity fully redeemed; but in his accomplishment as gaunt as a fire-swept building, of which nothing remains but its smoke-blackened shell . . .

The austere has its place; but may God forgive the devastating if unintended cruelty of that, and the way it battered one hurt soul I know back from the tender hands of Jesus!

Sensitiveness to beauty and sorrow, that "black heap" which lifts itself so hugely "and makes its wide entreaty to the sky." And then sensitiveness to situations, if I may put it so; that sensitiveness which we sometimes call tact and common sense. Not the kind of thing of which a friend of mine once said, "Three generations of tact make a liar!" But just ordinary susceptibility to the proper, the decent, and the fit. No use pretending that a man cannot help being tactless; he can. The trouble with tactless people well over half the time is that they are unwilling to put themselves out a little to be courteous and careful of the feelings of others. There are times, I am afraid, when even the best of us run along quite rudely in pursuit of our holy calling, with considerable disregard for pedestrians. It occurs to us that perhaps this will be overlooked as a sign of our preoccupation. And it is the sign of nothing but a callus. I remember one lad whom I advised, as he entered on his new field, to cultivate a certain woman of the parish. She had been disgruntled for a number of years, and not altogether without warrant. I told him she could do more to make his ministry there a success or a failure than any other one person. Within a month she was in my study telling me indignantly of how he had called on her and opened the conversation by remarking that he had understood from me that she was the most dangerous woman in the congregation! That may sound quite unbelievable, but it is quite true.

A man may not disport himself in the ministry pretty much as he pleases and presume upon the general good nature of the community. It matters whether or not he has good manners. It is vital to be unfailingly courteous and self-possessed; to dress, if not well, then with cleanliness; to be prompt in his correspondence—there are ministers whose desks are dead-letter offices; to be habitually as diligent, at least, as his average parishioner, up at a reasonable hour, and not a squanderer of time at baseball games and movies; *giving no offense in anything, that the ministry be not blamed* (II Corinthians 6:3, A.V.); with wisdom enough to exert a scrupulous care in business matters, not to make unnecessarily too sudden a change in any of the affairs of his congregation, never to move with small minorities. I could go on no doubt for another hour, but that would be myself to lack both tact and common sense! *In all things ap-*

*proving ourselves as the ministers of God* (II Corinthians 6:4,
A.V.). We can master the ordinary amenities of life if we will,
instead of turning up our clerical nose at them, shrugging our
clerical shoulders, and saying to our clerical selves that such
things are of no moment.

And now I am going to be bold enough to add that none of
these virtues, qualities, traits—call them what you will—is of
any lasting moment without that other which crowns them all,
humility. Where will you find it coupled with such passionate
sincerity as here in Ephesians (3:8)?

Less than the Least of All Saints

*as I am, this
grace was vouchsafed me.* Or again, *though I am the foremost
of sinners, I obtained mercy, for the purpose of furnishing
Christ Jesus with the chief illustration of his utter patience* (I
Timothy 1:15, 16). This is no crouching, no rubbing of the
hands by some Uriah Heep. Listen: *What I am is plain . . . to
your own conscience. . . . It is all the doing of the God who has
reconciled me to himself . . . and permitted me to be . . . an
envoy for Christ. . . . By great endurance, by suffering, by
troubles, by calamities, by lashes, by imprisonment; mobbed,
toiling, sleepless, starving; . . . with the weapons of integrity
for attack or for defense, amid honour and dishonour, amid
evil report and good report, an "imposter,"* I hear, *but honest,
"unknown"* you think *but well-known, dying, but here I am
alive, chastened but not killed, grieved but always glad, a "pau-
per"*—so say you—*but the means of wealth to many, without a
penny*—as many of you would put it—*but possessed of all* (II
Corinthians 5:11, 18, 20; 6:4-10). There is no hiding about anywhere.

Humility does not mean running oneself down. You will find
none of that in Paul. It means an emptying of "this cask of self,
with a bung of self, seasoned in a well of self." It means a stand-

ing of one's own endless baggage out of the way, that good may
come.

> If thou couldst empty all thy self of self,
>     Like to a shell dishabited,
> Then might He find thee on the ocean shelf,
>     And say, "This is not dead"—
> And fill thee with Himself instead.
>
> But thou art all replete with self, very thou,
>     And hast such shrewd activity,
> That when He comes He says, "This is enow
>     Unto itself—'twere better let it be:
> This is so small and full, there is no room for me."[10]

Dr. Buttrick reminds us[11] of the famous picture in the
Boston Public Library which shows Sir Galahad approaching
the Siege Perilous, that high seat whereon the motto ran, "He
who sits herein shall lose himself." And the knights round
about lift their sword-hilts in the sign of the Cross, as an angel
draws aside the scarlet drapery, and a voice seems to beat its
wings through the very air. *He who loses his life for my sake
will find it* (Matthew 10:39). That is humility. There is no
fawning, no discounting of one's gifts. Jesus said of himself,
you will remember, that he was meek and lowly; yet will
he utter solemn words that seem to crowd over on God: *He
who has seen me has seen the Father* (John 14:9). *You have
heard the saying . . . but I tell you . . .* (Matthew 5:38, 39,
et passim). There was no crawling out of the sun, no pretense of poverty. It was the selfless ministry of eternal love. *I
lay down my life for the sheep* (John 10:15). To this we are
called, and may God pity the proud among us!

I can think of no more insidious or deadly foe than self-esteem, the habit so many people have of being "starched even before they are washed." Yet I would hazard the guess that this

is peculiarly the sin par excellence of the clergy. It is a dark presence in the cellar of every man's life; we more than others should recognize its devious ways and keep ourselves as best we may from stroking it. Of it spring jealousies, bitterness, gossip, professionalism, the conceit of wisdom, ambition—which last is all right in Greek, but in Latin means a perfect willingness to be on both sides of any proposition at once! From sermons on the surpassing dignity of the human soul, spring all too often contemptuous references to others from whom we differ; from sermons on the freedom of conscience, strange assertions of the infallibility of our own position; from sermons on good will, queer outbursts of an evil temper against all opposite opinion.[12] From self-esteem spring controversy, narrowness, and self-sufficiency, so that the poor people who come to hear of Christ, as another has said, hear only of you.[13] Dr. Hutton in *That the Ministry Be Not Blamed* tells of a young man who began his discourse with these words: "In that important work of Cervantes, *Don Quixote,* . . . or, as I suppose you would call it, *Don Quix-ot* . . . "! The title of an ambitious book of the Middle Ages comes often to remind me of many a rotund and Sunday effort of my own. The title was *De Rebus Omnibus et Ceteris!* "Nothing," remarked Sainte-Beuve, "so resembles a hollow as a swelling."

Samuel Butler, in his *Way of All Flesh,* whether justly or unjustly the reader would no doubt hesitate to say, portrays what he supposes Mendelssohn's state of mind to have been on a certain occasion. I give it to you not as a righteous judgment, but as a skillful taking off, as one would take off an etching from the press, of our own shrewd and stealthy selves. In speaking of the Uffizi Gallery in Florence, Mendelssohn had said:

I sought out my favorite armchair and enjoyed myself for a couple of hours. This is a spot where a man feels his own insignificance and may well learn to be humble.

Writes Butler:

I wonder how many chalks he gave himself for having sat two hours on that chair. I wonder how often he looked at his watch to see if his two hours were up. I wonder how often he told himself that he was quite as big a gun, if the truth were known, as any of the men whose works he saw before him, how often he wondered whether any of the visitors were recognizing him and admiring him for sitting such a long time in the same chair, and how often he was vexed at seeing them pass him by and take no notice of him. But perhaps if the truth were known his *two hours* was not quite two hours.

I have never come across a better description of the narcissus mind in its unsophisticated and primitive estate! Men in the garb but not in the habit of humility who glance at their natural face in a mirror, but go not off, neither forget they what they thought themselves to be (James 1:23, 24). Men who are sure of God, in a condescending sort of fashion; define and so belittle Him, with more familiarity and freedom, said Leslie Stephens once, than any scientist would allow himself in the discussion of a black beetle under a showcase with a pin through its belly. They know all the answers, or so it would seem. A group of students in a theological seminary somewhere south of the Mason-Dixon Line said to me on one occasion that they had not had a visiting lecturer for many years who would even think of saying, "I don't know." Men who can prove to you jauntily that pain is necessary in the economy of this strange world, especially if the pain is yours; distribute blame with a generous hand but are niggardly with their praise. They have been shielded so long from frank criticism that they are unable to stand it any more. They have been so long the center of their parish that now they expect special consideration as their due. *Who singles you out, my brother?* (I Corinthians 4:7, 9)

And there is but one cure: solemnly and steadily to remember

Whose we are, and Whom we serve. *Knowing that he had come from God and was going to God,*—with such knowledge what would you do?—*he rose from table, laid aside his robe, and tied a towel round him, then poured water into a basin, and began to wash the feet of the disciples* (John 13:3, 4). What if ours, too, were a love willing to gird itself in that great name? A love willing to stoop because it comes from a throne to its task, and when its task is done goes to a throne again? A love that can afford to be lowly because it is great?

The releasing power of that high loyalty, which delivers one as well from the crippling sense of inferiority as from the devastating subtleties of pride, came over me one evening as I unexpectedly stood in a pulpit where Kagawa was to have stood and found myself facing the great audience which had gathered to hear him. In that moment a flood of self-consciousness swept down on me. I think I could have stammered and given it up had not a thought blazed suddenly in my mind, that after all I was not taking the place of Kagawa but of Jesus Christ. My hands to him for hands, there and always, and my lips for his Word! It happened more quickly than I can tell; but that flash of realization gave me my freedom.

There will be no questioning, writes Kierkegaard, as to whether I have won men; no questioning as to whether I have gained some earthly advantage; no questioning about what results I have produced, or whether I may have produced no results at all, or whether loss and the sport that others made of me were the only results I have produced. No, eternity will release me from one and all of such foolish questions. If it should so happen that in this talk I have spoken the truth, then I shall be questioned no further about this matter.[14]

*With me it is a very small thing that I should be judged of you, or of man's judgment: yea, I judge not mine own self. . . . He that judgeth me is the Lord* (I Corinthians 4:3, 4, A.V.). *I am eager to satisfy him* (II Corinthians 5:9).

Perhaps a few of us will have to wait until some genuine humiliation comes to trample us under foot. I can recall many an hour when God has taken me thoroughly at my word as I have prayed before going into the pulpit, "Not to my glory, but to Thine"; and has removed my glory from the picture so completely that the only shreds left must have been His! May our heart and our soul rejoice that day in our own stumbling!

Gentlemen, anything—anything—if only we may walk humbly with our God! As James Reid, that dear preacher of Eastbourne, England, once said to me, "It doesn't matter—it doesn't matter at *all* what becomes of *us!*" How would it be if we here were really to understand that, and under the spell of this life which was lived in Galilee, and may be lived whenever we will in us, make now our humble dedication?

There is an overwhelming body of truth in the intellectual
armories of Christendom which has only to be rightly used to
ensure a change of heart and mind throughout the world.

ALFRED NOYES, "The Edge of the Abyss"
*Fortune Magazine,* October, 1942

🗡🗡🗡🗡🗡🗡🗡🗡🗡🗡🗡🗡🗡🗡🗡🗡🗡🗡🗡🗡🗡🗡🗡🗡🗡🗡🗡🗡🗡🗡🗡🗡🗡🗡🗡🗡🗡🗡🗡🗡🗡🗡🗡

# Chapter 3

## THE WEAPONS OF MY WARFARE

🗡🗡🗡🗡🗡🗡🗡🗡🗡🗡🗡🗡🗡🗡🗡🗡🗡🗡🗡🗡🗡🗡🗡🗡🗡🗡🗡🗡🗡🗡🗡🗡🗡🗡🗡🗡🗡🗡🗡🗡🗡🗡🗡

*The weapons of my warfare,* writes the apostle, *are divinely
strong* (II Corinthians 10:4). Suppose we ask ourselves directly
at this point what they are. If preaching, or indeed any witness to the majesty and glory of God that a man can offer, is
the effectual mediation through personality of the truth as it is
in revelation and in experience, then at once, to give us at least
our direction, certain definitive statements should be set down
with regard to the scope and bearing of that truth.

Very clearly, without making it necessary for anybody *to
read between the lines* (II Corinthians 1:13), Paul indicates
the purpose which he feels himself appointed to serve. It is his
commission, as it is ours,

To Promote Obedience to the Faith*

not just be-
cause obedience would be a good thing, but because the gospel
is manifestly a matter of life and death. *I want you to understand my deep concern* (Colossians 2:1). *God is my witness that
I yearn for you all* (Philippians 1:8).

Surely, under such pressure as that, no one will allow himself
to squander his energies on trifling matters, on the circumfer-
ential, the eccentric, the cursory. *I take every project prisoner
to make it obey Christ* (II Corinthians 10:5). It has been well
pointed out that "the most brilliant handling of a trifle is only
trifling."[1] No warning could have been more appropriate to the
years of my early ministry. Week after week the Christian pulpit seemed to be under the spell of the casual and the frag-
mentary. I can remember being uneasily conscious many a time
that what I was saying and laboring so hard to say was peripheral. One arrow after another seemed to be sticking in the outer-
most rim of the target. Typical of the prevailing mood of that
whole generation was the newspaper assignment given a young
woman reporter to stop every man she met on the street to find
whether he wore pajamas or a nightgown. Mr. Hansen of *The
Herald Tribune* bears witness to the fact that he was once told
to visit a university and ask if an egg could be unscrambled.
The professor talked for an hour on entropy, the "Carnot prin-
ciple," and the second law of thermodynamics, explaining why
not. Scores of us were busy grubbing our message from the situations that confronted us. We were ready to regard eternity as
more or less superfluous while we did the best we could with
time! Texts were frequently broken off almost anywhere—
when texts were used at all; like that which was ironically suggested to the young curate, "Hang all the law and the prophets."[2] Our subjects more than once had to do with the latest

* Romans 1:5.

novel, perhaps with the most recent development in philosophy or science. And always there was the week's budget of news, social, political, international, calling throughout its length and breadth for ministerial analysis. On a Saturday morning in *The New York Times* the following appeared among the oracles on the religious page:

The inaugural address of President Roosevelt will be commented on in many sermons tomorrow. Pastors will also refer to the fact that next Saturday will be the birthday of the Chief Executive. Ministers will speak of the automobile strike, and at least one clergyman will preach on "The Sit-Down Strike in the Churches."

And I dare say the dire prophecy was fulfilled. But to whose eternal welfare? As material for magazine articles much of it was excellent. Some of it actually got in! But very little of it was intrinsically fit for the pulpit.

I submit to you that at best we have but meager opportunity to confront human life with this momentous Word of God, whispered down out of heaven, and in the long crying of man's soul incarnate from the earth. What possible excuse is there for throwing such opportunity as we have to the winds by sorting out in public the flotsam and jetsam of a restless, kaleidoscopic world?

Make the Very Most of Your Time

So said Paul, from the midst of evil days (Colossians 4:5; Ephesians 5:16). We are here to speak to our age from the ages, of *the fathomless wealth of Christ,* of *the full sweep of the divine wisdom, in terms of the eternal purpose* (Ephesians 3:8, 10, 11). We are to set within the circle of that great light all judgments and duties, all love and hope and life, that when we are done there might stand the hills of a celestial country against the sky, with a kind of foreverness about all the days as if they were still trailing through the dust of this earth, each its own cloud of glory from the God who is their home.

Nor should preaching be allowed to squander its energies on anything less than the whole man. It must not commit itself solely to the elucidation of difficulties, however learned and religious; to the constant stirring up of enthusiasms, however righteous and profound; to the perpetual reinforcement of some earnest purpose, however altruistic and lofty. The function of preaching lies in no one of these three directions; it lies in all of them together: "to teach and to inspire; to prove and to persuade; to paint and to compel."

Whatever, therefore, the actual subject of a sermon may be, granted the loftiness and dignity of its reference, its matter must speak to the *understanding* of men and women in terminologies and categories that are intellectually respectable. Not that the preacher should pounce at once upon every fresh interpretation of life and the world which science seems to make possible and philosophy would suggest; but that at least he should not forever cling to outworn patterns and fearfully dispense an ancient vocabulary,—in the manner of that fabled bird which flies backwards because it does not care much where it is going; it wants only to know where it has been. The salvation of the race does not depend primarily on its holding fast to something; the salvation of the race depends on its adventurous faith in him who once looked out on an order tumbling like ours half-a-hundred ways into ruin and said, *As my Father has continued working to this hour, so I work too* (John 5:17). The mind of God is no Lot's wife on the plains of Sodom, hardened now into a spectral figure. The mind of God is a cloud and smoke by day and the shining of a flaming fire within the night. What terrifies me is not the man who tries to think when he gets inside the covers of the Bible, but the man who doesn't,—good people who never bother with adding knowledge to their goodness, who mean well and do not know what they mean. Some of them are self-styled liberals, to whom creeds do not matter; if only you will throw yourself in alongside and work hard for the Kingdom of God, you don't need much information about either God or the Kingdom. Many of them are conservatives, they aren't sure about what; but they do join lustily in the hymns, hymns that are often enough chock-full of moral and intellectual dishonesty, hugging words that have lost their content, putting to a tune their hope for things they do not hope for.

> Jerusalem, my happy home,
> Would God I were in thee!

But not yet a while! The janitor of some city church when they asked him how he got along so well with so many men and women telling him what to do, said, "Well I just throw my mind into neutral and go where I'm pushed!" *He that hasteth with his feet sinneth, and the soul that is without knowledge, it is not good* (Proverbs 19:2, 3, A.V.). There is a claim which God has on the minds of men. In the first chapter of Proverbs, Wisdom cries aloud: *Because I have called, and ye refused, I will mock when your fear cometh* (Proverbs 1:24, 26, A.V.). The kind of Christianity that goes to pieces under pressure is the kind that limps into the presence of Almighty God a partial, crippled thing, with less than its whole self, because its mind, for one reason or another, is missing.

The sermon must speak to the understanding, but no less must it speak to the *heart*. During Lent of 1943, some twenty of us on the West Side of New York were preaching each Sunday on uniform themes from Second Isaiah. I remember very vividly the sermon I wrote on The Necessity of Religion. I tore it up because it left even me, that child of my brain, with the feeling that religion was necessary,—so what? There was nothing for it but to throw the emphasis where it belonged, on the appealing-ness of God in Christ. To rely on the emotions is demoralizing; to shun them is stupid and impossible. It may be that sentimentality, which is sentiment that has slipped its leash, has come near destroying our American Christianity. I believe it has. Jesus recoiled from it as if it were a bottomless pit at his very feet. But we are still whole numbers, and we shall never work as fractions. You cannot divide us as you would real estate. Allow our emotions to knock about freely in this lot, give our minds something to do in that, and in number three turn our wills loose like a herd of bulls. If a man does not operate all together, he would better not operate. We are religious with the sum total of our lives, or we are simply not religious! Christopher Morley writes of a good book what could with equal force be set down of a good sermon: "It ought to come like Eve from somewhere near the third rib; there ought to be a heart beating in it."[3] A sermon that is "all forehead doesn't amount to much." "Moonlight preaching ripens no harvests."[4]

So, too, because we are whole numbers and not fractions, the sermon must speak to the *wills* of men, lest everything fritter out into nothing but a hope, making ineffectual gestures to human life from beyond the confines of human history. No theology, however pessimistic and full of despair, can gainsay the possibility of that change, individual and corporate, which Christianity came into the world to accomplish. No academic discussion about where the Kingdom of God is located can relieve us of undertaking to locate here as much of it as we can. It takes no idealist, no utopian dreamer, to set his face against the "unnecessary necessity" of living in a hell on earth. There strikes an hour when *what is old is gone, the new has come* (II Corinthians 5:17). If the Christian religion cannot make good at that point, it cannot make good anywhere. There is a victory of God in the human soul, and there is a victory of God in human relations. "The demand of the Real," says Nels Ferré, "is that present realization be found wanting"; but no less that "present actuality be increasingly transformed."[5] "When the Church lowers its demands to the alleged needs of secular society," he goes on, "it becomes a light set under a bushel, salt good for nothing." The pull on the Church is the pull on history. It is not the pull of an ideal. It is the pull of God. To this I shall ask the privilege of returning.

Meanwhile, to go home and leave things there as they were is to change the truth into a lie, and our grim world into a shadow. If we are to be saved, we are to be saved to some purpose, not to argue or to feel, but to risk and to fashion. That's what Christianity is for. It was never a philosophy. It was never a code of ethics. It was always the offer of power. You took it or you left it. Precisely at the point where you liked the old least you could have the new. Up and down the streets for twenty centuries the gospel has been hawking its wares. That is what it is about. And it is about nothing else.

For this reason we have come, I suppose quite inevitably, to use the phrase "preaching for a verdict." It is not, I dare suggest, the happiest phrase we could use. There is about it far too much of the argumentative, the evidential, the forensic, to express the full, true genius of the Christian pulpit. Verdicts are too often won by mere brilliance, even by trickery. Nor are they always rendered in accordance with the facts. And having been rendered, they have to be executed by somebody else. I sometimes think we should do better perhaps to borrow not from the courts but from courtship. There is a knocking at the door that wants an answer. A quiet talk. A question is asked. And mind and heart and will together are shut up not alone to a true decision but to a life, *till Christ be formed within you* (Galatians 4:19).

Preaching, then, should not be allowed to squander its energies on trifles, or on anything less than the whole man. Neither should it be allowed to squander its energies on anything less than the whole Truth. *I am a minister of the church,* writes Paul to the Colossians out of his prison house (1:25), *by the divine commission which has been granted me in your interests, to make*

### A Full Presentation of God's Message

It is ours, as preachers of a Word that is in our charge but does not belong to us, to be constantly on the alert lest we find ourselves by insensible degrees falling into the habit of laying such unremitting stress on some one aspect or another of Christian thought or practice as to defeat both the symmetry and the purpose of the whole. There are those of us, for example, who seem never to have found our way out of the Old Testament into the New, out of law into grace; and there are others of us who never once run out hardily from the shelter of that grace into the rigors again of eternal law. Here perhaps on the Presbyterian side of the public square in almost any town one may find justice without mercy; there on the Lutheran side, which I know better, mercy without justice. Down this street almost every Sunday religion spends all its time trying to get into politics and economics and has a very hard job making any headway. Around the corner on that street it does its level best with the aid of poetry to keep out of everything that might matter and exhausts its half-hour marching seven times around some Jericho long since evacuated. The gospel is not patchwork: it is a living organism. It is not to be separated into its component parts and dispensed piecemeal. It is to come into human life entire. There is only one thing in the pulpit more important than telling the truth, and that is telling the whole truth. Though it may be added by way of caution that we all have not one Sunday but quite a few in which to do it!

With this in mind, and in clear view of all that has been said, may I stress the fact that preaching of whatever type must of necessity, to be true preaching, articulate itself ultimately in Christian doctrine? Fundamentally every sermon must rely for its strength and carrying power on the accuracy and force with which it presents, portrays, and interprets the great, central facts of the Christian religion. It is simple folly to talk of preaching that is practical without being theoretical, or inspirational without being theological. Practice, if it is wise, has a way of rooting itself in theory; and inspiration without theology is like the grin of the Cheshire cat. You will remember how completely bewildered Alice was in her Wonderland to see the grin lingering when the cat was gone. Dr. Luccock has aptly illustrated the point by quoting the inscription set over the entrance to that amphitheatre in Beverly Hills, California, which was dedicated some time ago to the housing of an American Passion Play: Here among our eternal hills, so it ran, we build a shrine, sans creed, sans dogma, inspiring all mankind. Which, remarks Dr. Luccock, is a good trick if you can do it.[6] Actually, of course, any religion that boasts of being creedless is either misrepresenting the facts or writing its own epitaph. It is upon the eternal nature of things that human destiny depends. It is on his knowledge of and his faith in that eternal nature of things that a man must live his life, fashion his religion, and find what he can of power and peace. The state of her lodger's exchequer, writes Chesterton, is not so important to the landlady as is his total view of the universe. And why not? At bottom all conduct is some philosophy gone off on an errand. And so are all sermons that get anywhere. "Skimmed theology" will nourish no great saints![7]

## I

What, then, is to be the content of our preaching? I believe there are three chief heads and accents under which we have to move as under banners if the sermon is to be whole and central and true; because it seems to me there are three facts which taken together constitute the very cutting edge of our dilemma.

First of all, the world apparently has got bigger than God. Certainly that is how it looks to a good many people. Our spiritual forefathers there in the Old Testament had a God they were bold enough to picture. He walked in a garden once, and somehow they could feel that He was quite within it. When they went outside they took Him with them. They journeyed over into Palestine, to follow the sequence of the story as it is written; and their ideas grew larger. Down into Egypt and back home; away into exile. He was of considerable stature now and of great glory. Read Second Isaiah for the sheer magnificence of its imagery: the jeweler's scales in which He weighed the hills as dust and the seas as the moisture of His breath. The room they had for Him was growing.

Then came Jesus of Nazareth, and God was no longer to be bound to any place or to any time. He was a Spirit, *neither on this mountain nor at Jerusalem* (John 4:21). Every crisis of the human epic was met with that expanding image. Paul would have it that salvation was for the Gentiles too. There would be Greek Christians and Roman Christians. The Jews leaned back. That was going too far. The apostle swept them aside with his question: *Who are you, my man, to speak back to God?* (Romans 9:20) And the years plunged on, leaving them behind. There was no housing of God anywhere. The councils of the Church framed huge definitions in which to keep men comfortable for a while; but God broke through, once, and again, and a third time. Four hundred years ago He broke through in the Reformation. Then cautiously, trembling at what they had done, theologians got busy to compass Him once more and bring Him within the confines of some roomier doctrine. But none of it was big enough to hold Him. He refuses to stay in our categories.

And that is where you and I are standing. We have discovered whatever there is in the world to discover,—except the ice caps, a little of them, and the origin of life, and the nature of matter, with some other minor details which we are just now in process of cleaning up,—while here alongside of it we have been discovering the universe. Time is longer than we thought and space is wider. We run out toward it with notions to which we have been diligently adding for two thousand years, and still they don't fit! We look back at the thought our elders had of God, and build a wing out here and an ell out there, precisely as New England farmers used to do with their houses; but build as they would those houses were still dwarfed against the stately march of the mountains and the far winding of the river. We struggle with such words as "infinite" and "eternal"; but now that the astronomers and mathematicians have charted their "awesome sweep" they stagger us. We find ourselves unable to worship a "table of logarithms." It is not easy, wrote Gaius Glenn Atkins, to fill the dark spaces between the stars with a sovereign personality.[8] Some of us have begun to wonder if God can care and prayer can count. Look at the world; what kind of rule does that reflect? Besides, there are so many of us! I myself never have any trouble with the doctrine of immortality except in the subway rush-hour! There are such teeming millions gazing out into the "grim void of that cosmic order where light itself grows old in its journey from star to star!"

And the bearing of all this? Simply that we are under compulsion before all else to exalt

The Wisdom and Knowledge of God*

The modern sermon, if we plan to make it significant and effective, must give to men a greater God than any they have yet imagined for themselves! Most of the trouble people have with their faith

* Romans 11:33.

comes not of knowing too much about life or about the world, but of knowing too little about God. Once more, a year or so ago, Mr. Einstein publicly deplored this faith of ours in a personal Deity; supposing, according to the newspaper account, that most of us worship a distinguished old gentleman made in our image. Might we not reasonably ask that a man wade through Christian theology far enough to be aware that if the belief in a personal God means anything, it means only that whatever else God is over and above a person, He is at least that? Personality is the category to which Christians believe He willingly reduced Himself in order to be known by finite creatures. It is His least denominator common with us. Minus all the rest that we do not know about, He is a loving, intelligent will, brooding over the universe, working out within history and beyond it His own inscrutable but sovereign and unchangeable purpose. All we can ever do is to throw our words out, as Matthew Arnold once said, at a reality immeasurably beyond our power of expression. *Lo, these are parts of his ways: but how little a portion is heard of him?* (Job 26:14 A.V.). Meanwhile can they ever come to know Him who make no effort and take no pains? I have never discovered the secret of knowing any of my friends, even, without putting my back into it. It is not a different faith humanity needs; it is a larger faith.

Dr. Adam Burnet told me a few summers back of an experience he had had in the last war. He was standing one evening not far from the tall spire of a village church. For some unknown reason the firing on both sides had died down, and the setting sun rode red at the rim of the world. Suddenly, a lone shell came screaming through the twilight, and the top half of the tower blew apart with a deafening roar. Almost simultaneously a covey of birds which had been nesting there rose slowly above the smoke and the flying bits of stone, hovered in the air for a moment, and then settled quietly back. He said it seemed like the greatness of God to him, lifting over the ruin and the pain; only to brood down, after men had done their worst, and nest again silently close to the earth.

Is it not so with us? We have been stirring up an awful racket down here with light-years and relativity. In John Dewey's mind a doubt explodes; and all the philosophers sit around in *The Christian Century* to watch the pieces fly. "Here," cries someone, "push God away with this measurement, tie Him hand and foot with that law. Take the mystery of evil yonder. Why did *my* son have to die? There isn't anything in prayer but auto-suggestion." It has been a fearful clatter. And there, always, when we have done,

> Above the smoke and stir of this dim spot
> Which men call earth,

above the dust of all our little qualms and battles, there is God. He is just greater than we thought. Too great to be pushed away into space somewhere; greater than the pain which seems to contradict Him and the loss you think He cannot make up; great enough to have you for a friend, and to care about it, and to listen when you whisper to Him whatever it is that is in your heart. There is Jesus' kind of God: great enough to mark a sparrow's fall, lifting like that covey of birds till the clamor of your soul is still, then settling down over all this bewildered place with His peace.

Here certainly lies something of the significance of Karl Barth. He was bound to unveil for his generation the distance between God and man, and to remind us that "our Father after all is in Heaven":

Were we to hear only of a God who, fortunately for Him, measures up to our rule and is able to do what we can also do ourselves without Him, what need have we of such a god? Whenever the church has told man of such a tiresome little god it has grown empty. That radical daring, our yearning for the living God, will not be gain-said. It lives when and wherever the Church discovers the Bible. Men's souls will then come into their own. But the Church must really discover it. Oh that it were given the Church really to understand her misery and her grandeur! To understand that men really do hunger and thirst for the truth of the Bible because they yearn to break through the whole array of our gods into the presence of the true and living God! Then the Church would be transformed. From a place half tedious and half solemn, which it is so largely, it would become today a place where men are roused and made fully awake; yea, it would be changed into a living fountain to quench the thirst of our age.[9]

Certainly, among other things, we ought to call a halt to all our loose talk about seeking Him. Loose talk has done Christianity incalculable harm. I have never heard that God was lost. If He is, then space and eternity are much too big for me to find Him in either of them. We speak of discovering His Kingdom, or bringing it, or doing something else with it; and half the time we have never even made approximately clear in our own minds what His Kingdom is. With the slightest provocation we run off from all attempts at disciplined thinking to wonder whose side He is on in the war, as if being on His side made no difference. Some of us even suggest that possibly He ought to stop the whole frightful business; though just how, without making moral imbeciles of us, is never quite clear. We press up to Him insistently with our little yardsticks. Solemn gentlemen mount the steps of solemn pulpits and tell us it is of no use to pray for rain[10] or for health or for safety in the midst of danger: it is of no use to pray for anything in fact except for moral courage and a better disposition,—though if the truth were known these too no doubt depend very largely on the state of your liver. Jesus Christ, poor man, talked of God as if He were a Father who knew folk's names; but that was the primitive religion of an early day when everything was neat and simple..

Now we have acquired the quantum theory and Planck's constant $h$. We have to quit being so childish. Besides, how can this thing, and something else, and that other thing,—how can these things be? If we cannot understand enough of it we throw it over. God has to act pretty much as we would have Him act, or we'll know the reason why and have nothing to do with Him. The very idea of His embarking on some course that's unintelligible to us! And so we come to that last absurdity, a man denying God because he, the man, cannot seem to make sense of a number of things.

Writes a friend of mine, quite unconscious that the limitations are in himself, not in the object of his contemplation: "God is strangely contradictory. Has He a split personality? He gives man a free will but permits him to be conditioned by his environment and inheritance to a limited freedom. In some areas of his inner life he is enslaved and does not know it. God gives man freedom of choice but also thrusts him into a highly technical, intricate, and astronomical world without the information, experience, and judgment required to make sound decisions. God tells man: Ask, and ye shall receive; seek, and ye shall find; knock, and it shall be opened unto you. But in the midst of modern world conditions, how is man to know what to ask and whether he has heard God aright? How can finite man find solutions to his infinite problems? And why knock when the door remains shut in his face?"

Beyond these horizons of the human mind, within which God must strive as best He may to accommodate Himself, what if He were a greater God than any you and I even yet suppose? What if we had not even begun to know anything about Him, or His ways of working, or His plans, except that He loves us undiscourageably, as Jesus said? *What if,* asks Paul in a stately passage of Romans (9:22, 23). May I not ask it too? What if we do not quite see what He is about today and tomorrow, or why

He does what He does? Our notions may not be the only notions there are in the universe, or even the standard notions, by
which all the others must be judged. One of the chief services
which mathematics has rendered the human race, insists Dr.
Bell somewhere in one of his books, was to put "common
sense" where it belongs, on the topmost shelf next to the dusty
canister labeled "discarded nonsense." Why, asks W. P. Lemon
in *The Christian Century,* if, as some philosophers affirm, the
world is alogical at the very core; if "at the end of our knowledge we know God the unknown"; if "the highest cannot be
spoken,"—why should we be so hot on the heels of certitude?
The effort to bring the spiritual life down from the "stratos-
pheric" is dark from its own excess of light.[11]

Surely there is something significant about the present-day
weariness of people with their own home-made mental straight-
jackets. It is one of the characteristic marks of our time. Why is
it that the prophets of the New Order both in Germany and in
Japan have offered as a substitute for reason the most primitive
of patterns that gleefully contradict it,—in order to induce what
Otto Tolischus in his *Tokyo Record* calls "the warrior psychology of the savage tribe"?[12] Why is it not possible that the issue
for us as well lies not in that which is contrary to reason or prior
to it, but in that which is above it, within which are compre-
hended both its finiteness and its tragedy? *What human being,*
the apostle wants to know (I Corinthians 2:11), *can understand
the thoughts of a man, except the man's own inner spirit? So
too,* he concludes,

> No One Understands the Thoughts of God
>
> *except the*

*Spirit of God.* What if we do not quite see how His plan for our
lives would work out down here where by no choice of our own
we have come to live? What if we cannot quite conceive of doing the things He keeps insisting we should? Overcoming evil

with good, for instance, instead of forever trying to wipe it out
with its own weapons. Turning the other cheek, instead of letting the other fellow have it with our fist—both fists and both
feet, if we can manage to be unanimous! Maybe *we* are wrong.
I am confident of this: that if I understood Him I would do
well to doubt Him. Granted a Word of God to my soul, somewhere in its vastness, from the middle of this world where "the
veriest spider wrecks the mind,"[13] I shall be shaking my head.
Strive as He may, He can hardly accommodate Himself wholly
to my horizons.

People tell me that the doctrine of the Virgin Birth doesn't
fit our scientific conceptions. I ask you, What of it? They say
they do not like the idea of a bloody sacrifice. The immortality
of the soul doesn't seem to them very plausible. It must all
sound funny to God if He can get any time off from being sad.
Vega, that blue star right over your head on a summer's night,
sits squarely up there in space on nothing, and weighs God only
knows how much,—God and a few astronomers. That does not
seem plausible either. They warn me with a finger; they frown
at me. You must realize that we live in two worlds, the ideal
and the real. Over here Jesus was exactly right. Over there, it
will not work. Which means to me nothing but an ultimate
denial of the sovereignty of God. I know about relative values
and choices neither black nor white; but I find there no ground
for indulging in theft, if not once a day, then at least twice a
week! They ask what will become of justice if you take Christ's
way. I ask what became of it on Calvary. It may be that we
shall have to leave most of it where it was then. There seems at
the very least to be a tragic fallacy somewhere in our human
brand! Nothing seems to make an end of its vicious circle. It is
like a very saga of Helen, and Agamemnon, and Iphegenia, and
Clytemnestra, and Orestes: with nobody ever breaking through,
to do more than cancel the wrong with his pardon, to restore

and redeem the life that did it. We have never yet measured the justice that is in love, of which love is the only possible ground, the kind of love that undertakes to win back a lost creation in the only way there is to win it back, the pressure of its own hurt life leaning undefeated against the world. Say it is naïve. When you have puzzled your brains into a dead end, backed them against a wall, and tied them with knots, it is time to be naïve. There is a kind of naïveté about the gospel, and about the Kingdom of God, and about the children who enter it. Christianity at its best is the sense the heart makes. Perhaps our minds will never agree to it wholly, but God's mind and God's heart are one. And it is His sense that matters.

He is a God who may well be a mystery to us forever, except that in so far as we can guess at Him, He is like this carpenter from Nazareth. It came over me one day with the rush of a revelation, and the vastest thought I had ever had of Him in all my life seemed on the instant infinitesimal. A friend was talking to me of that age-old problem of human suffering. "Why does God allow it?" he asked. "This much I know," he answered himself. "I have seen a captain send one of his men, a dear friend of his, to certain death; and the man spent no time in asking why. He saluted and went. I do not know why, and I am not asking. I am just saluting, if that is my post. In God's name, can't we have the courage even of soldiers? He knows. So much I understand!" It was like a great tide rising, and I am still somehow on the crest of it. The majesty of God! Is that what Job means? *When I founded the earth, where were you then? Who helped to shut in the sea, when it burst from the womb of chaos? Have you ever roused the morning, given directions to the dawn? What path leads to the home of Light, and where does Darkness dwell? Have you seen the arsenals of the hail? Have showers a human sire? Who was the father of the dew?* (Job 38:4, 8, 12, 19, 22, 28) And Job laid his hand on

his lips. So did Paul, after he had wrestled with the ways of
Providence through three chapters of his letter to the Romans
(9, 10, 11), only to make very little sense out of any of it:
*O the depth of the riches both of the wisdom and knowledge
of God! How unsearchable are his judgments, and his ways
past finding out!* (Romans 11:33, A.V.) Shall we do as much?
Before the face of One Whose thoughts are not our thoughts,
neither are His ways our ways? Like Mr. Jefferson, writes
Albert Jay Nock in his *Diary of a Superfluous Man,* I have
always been content to "repose my head on that pillow of
ignorance which a benevolent Creator has made so soft for
us, knowing how much we should be forced to use it."

It is not another faith that we need; it is a greater faith. The
sermon, to be a sermon at all, to win for itself honor and a hearing, must bring to men the sense of that *aliquid immensum infinitumque* of which Cicero used to speak. Says John Bennett,
there are times when the very first word to be uttered about God
is not love, not personality, but mystery and transcendence.[14]
There *is* a "burden of the Eternal;" and unless it lies heavily on
a man's soul, there is no preaching.

> As the marsh-hen secretly builds on the watery sod,
> Behold I will build me a nest on the greatness of God:
> I will fly in the greatness of God as the marsh-hen flies
> In the freedom that fills all the space 'twixt the marsh and
>     the skies:
> By so many roots as the marsh-grass sends in the sod
> I will heartily lay me a-hold on the greatness of God.[15]

The world has not got bigger than He is. It has got bigger than
our idea of Him. And we have to climb.

Be Thou exalted, writes Augustine, O God, who wast made
flesh in her whom Thou didst make . . . Thou who didst
hunger for our sakes, thirst for our sakes, wast wearied on the
road for our sakes (does the Bread hunger, and the Fountain

thirst, and the Way get tired?), . . . Thou who didst sleep, yet, keeping Israel, dost not slumber; whom Judas sold, whom the Jews bought, yet did not possess; seized, bound, scourged, crowned with thorns, hung upon the tree, Thou dead, Thou buried, Be Thou exalted, O God, above the heavens, . . . and Thy glory above all the earth.[16]

## II

But we must move along. If the first head or accent of preaching in our day is to be the greatness and sovereignty of God, the second must be the tragic estate of the human soul. That, too, is determined for us, I think, not only by the unchanging character of the gospel itself, but also by the immediacies of our present situation.

Perhaps the most paradoxical of all the facts which confront us at the moment is that weird combination of self-esteem and self-contempt, of overweening pride coupled with a sense of cosmic insignificance, which, as I have already pointed out, marks the modern spirit. Psychologists have no great difficulty accounting for such a conflict when it exists in the individual. It is our old friend, the inferiority complex, with the defense mechanism which tries so hard to compensate for it. May I suggest here that the pattern is not altogether incapable of application to history?

Man at one time, of course, thought himself by all odds the most important bit of God's handiwork. It wasn't so difficult to believe that the Infinite Designer of all things would go out of His way for Abraham and counsel with Moses; for after all Abraham and Moses were stately folk. Even the poor peasant who listened on that hillside, drinking in the words of Jesus like some wayfarer of the desert dying of thirst, felt that those words were true words; and they made him sure that he *was* somewhat, and could afford to smile at the stars set there in the heavens for his pleasure! Slaves began to move about through the earth under the spell of them with a certain dignity. *Faith has come, and we are wards no longer; you are* All Sons of God

*by your faith in Christ Jesus . . . There is no room for Jew or Greek, there is no room for slave or freeman, there is no room for male and female. . . . It is because you are sons that God has sent forth the Spirit of his Son into your hearts crying Abba! Father!* (Galatians 3:25, 26, 28; 4:6)

But then the change set in. People lost their stature and turned into vassals again. Lords took over their lands and the church took over their thinking. Luther in his crude and sometimes bewildered fashion tried to aim a gallant blow at it; but life seems to have a dreadful genius for forging shackles faster than we can strike them off. By many a devious, willful way, in search of self-hood, we have missed it. Being the masses would not have made so much difference,—fooled by politicians, jockeyed about by government, exploited by money-grabbers,—if only we had not become at the same time "a fortuitous concourse of atoms," or "a disease of matter on the epidermis of a pigmy planet." We might be able to get along all right with economic materialism if only we did not have to surrender to reflexes! Being born in a hospital, as just one item of mass production, with a tag around your neck, so Charles Merz puts it, then after a while buried from parlor A, with music B and flower class C,—none of this by itself needs to worry anybody; but being psychoanalyzed on top of it into creatures of habit hardly fourteen years old—that is embarrassing.

So has most of our prestige slipped from us. Increased knowledge seems only to have subtracted from our happiness, with gadgets that cannot comfort us and toys that never seem able to make up the loss. We have undertaken to *fathom all mysteries* and found ourselves to be but *baffling reflections in a mirror* (I Corinthians 13:2, 12).

And I wonder if that is not why this imperious nature of ours boils over and we set about assuming some fictitious importance. We are Aryans, believe it or not. We bluster and wear gold braid. We pile up a big balance in the bank, purchase wide acres, hail from New York, Miami, and Bar Harbor all at once, pretend, fight. Like some prince of the blood who has despised his rightful inheritance and shut himself out of it, taken him a house in a mean and gossipy village, and there tried to find some misshapen outlet for the royal habit of his mind. It would be a tragedy of the first water to watch him sink away into peevish madness, from a throne to a broken chair by the stove in a smelly little post office, snarling and snapping at his neighbours. It is what happens inevitably when these human lives of ours, fashioned for God, sell their birthright for one of the petty slaveries of the world. If we could take a continuous motion picture of them, in which the years would be minutes and the months seconds, flash it against a screen, and look at the disintegration going on with the speed of melting snow, I think we could not stand it.

Should you ever want a sample of the sorrows of Jesus, there you are. He saw the soul of man, created for grandeur, taking out its glory in ridiculous little claims, firing its guns, feeding its hunger with greed and lust and a taste for power, improving itself emptier and emptier, until it brings down around its ears the grim ruin of a broken world. The passion for self-annihilation, which always seems to signal the last stages of man's suicidal pride, becomes almost demonic. A sense of abysmal futility, not to be dispelled by this shot-in-the-arm excitement and stimulus of war, settles down over the human spirit. And you have in front of you, ready-made, one of the prime objectives of Christian preaching.

The plain fact of revelation is of course that man's real and essential dignity took shape when God set out to do the most magnificent thing even He could think of doing. He set out to fashion a life with the infinite vistas of His own life hidden in it. That was the richest thing He could lay His hands on as He looked about among His treasures. On and on He wrought to give it grandeur while He gave it freedom. And it used its freedom to wrench itself away from Him. He told it by seer and martyr and Book how it could get up and out in a world like this; and it spread its legs apart and stood against Him. Then in this man of Galilee He showed it; and nobody ever since has been able to do anything but wish it were so. He tried to win it with His pain, looked it steadily in the eyes, and died for it. He had known He would all along. That's how He had worked things out, weaving the pattern whole there in eternity. A smile shining through His tears, because He was happy with His dream; there could not have been a better; sad only for what man kept doing to it. But He would go on. And time and human history are all we can see of that on-going. They are its underside.

This is the story in brief that the Bible tells; and with it the Christian faith stands or falls. All the way through the Book the movement is away from the tribe and the group to this stark figure or that, daring to get to his feet, shaken loose before the Eternal: ignorant, his days like the grass, puny against the terrible majesty of creation, brutal—the Jews bore in their own flesh the marks of his brutality; and yet for all that, there on the narrow strip of beach between the vastness of the sky and the waves of godless inhumanity that poured over them, they held on to their defiant faith in him, called him great, said he was only a little lower than the angels, a little less than divine, wondered at him, God-crowned as he was with glory and honor, disentangled him slowly from the crowd, set him alone before his Maker and left him there.

Man's common dust, these writers knew, was sifted out of the most amazing grandeur. You will see it many a time, as they had seen. Hopes that suddenly streak up out of the slums like the banners of the morning, red courage in pale little clerks that you may never match, a will tottering with age that can be smashed to its knees only to struggle back on its feet and shake itself and march again. That is what makes humanity human, and a man a man: not his groveling, but his groping; not his crawling, but his standing on tiptoe sometimes for a beauty that is beyond him, and letting his heart break but he will have it. The Bible cannot get over that.

Nor can it ever forget that we are capable too of falling away into a bottomless abyss. It points to something that is lordly about us all, with the boldest, hungriest hopes; but to something, too, that is terrible, willing at times, when the devils inside begin stirring, to take the best we have ever seen and curse it and nail it to a tree. Whatever we are, the dimensions somehow seem to be gigantic, always hung up somewhere half-way between heaven and hell. The pity of the last four centuries is that we have consistently distorted and misinterpreted our reading of them, missed almost completely the significance of that immense contradiction, and missing it have contemptuously tossed aside the religion which no longer seemed necessary as we dug ourselves more and more deeply into the pit.

But that is not all. This homeless being, so tragically endowed, fleeing away from good

In the Thraldom of Sin*

and not content with evil, is capable of moving about in the companionship of the Eternal, with fleeting glimpses of God, or so he thinks, that make him catch his breath. Maybe like the Jews you will have

* Romans 7:14.

to fight your way up through tragedy to get any real hold of it; but they set it down in the Book with utter certainty. Nothing about him was more significant. It was the most real fact in the universe, the seal and signature of the ultimate, far more meaningful than the bare and outward pattern of the world.[17] With things as they were, it was not always a solace and a comfort. It hounded people, too. It twisted them again and again out of their old worn paths, harried them, made them uneasy. They ran to it for refuge against the wicked: *Thy love is high as heaven . . . thy justice is like mighty mountains, thy judgments are like the deep sea. To thee men come for shelter in the shadow of thy wings; they have their fill of choice food in thy house, the stream of thy delights to drink; for life's own fountain is within thy presence, and in thy smile we have the light of life.* (Psalm 36:5–9) But the smile seemed ever and again to turn threateningly into a frown. A man would look up for succor, and then perforce he would have to look down at his own naked wretchedness. The company he had to keep was too great for him; he never could get out of his eyes the glaring inconsistencies of his own being. There were the clean heights to which he felt himself called; and there was the deep abyss within, where the glory kept shining from beyond his world.

Walter Horton has put for us this whole huge paradox in a striking figure.

A living plant derives its whole being ultimately from the sun. . . . But every plant has a spontaneity of its own, whereby it uses the common gift of radiance from above in a manner peculiar to itself. Some plants turn solar energy into flowers that reflect the colors of the solar spectrum, and fruits that sustain life; others turn it into poison. . . . It is so also with mankind. Man is compact of light, and light alone; there is nothing dark or evil in his original composition. But noblest of all the good gifts which God has showered upon His human creatures is a gift of spontaneity far higher than a plant's, a veritable power to create which, within finite bounds, images the infinite power of the Creator. This creative gift is a gift of light, but man can use it for works of darkness. He probably began so using it as soon as he became a man. . . . He tripped and fell over the very first step that led him up above the level of brutality, and he has done the same at every step on the way from savagery to higher civilization. . . . The result is something more terrible than any one of us could create by himself. There is gradually built up, in the midst of God's fair earth, a "City of Dreadful Night," walled about with thick darkness, so that God's light cannot get in.[18]

It is precisely at this moment that we turn the page and come to the New Testament. If you want anybody to know why God had to get into the world with His hands and feet, had to walk down the stairs of heaven to Bethlehem with that child in His arms, here it is. Something had to be done about this strange and broken creature with the staring eyes that felt Him near and shouted for joy; then shuddered and wished Him far away. This ugly, turbulent creature, so dreary and splendid, so princely and full of heartache, so ineffably gay and immutably piteous! Herein lies the rationale of the Christian gospel. From under the brows of the Nazarene, the Eternal God looked long into man's tragic soul; spoke to him,—it was like the first sane speech a madman hears when he is clear of his madness; said radiant things that swept across his clouded mind as the sunshine sweeps across a meadow; took him confidently by the hand, quite sure of the future; led him to a cross and died for him there with a gallant whisper, *To day shalt thou be with me in paradise!* (Luke 23:43 A.V.)

We think of the evil that took Jesus to the cross as a problem to be explained. We incline to hold one or the other of half a dozen theories to account for it and to help us get rid of as much of the responsibility as we can. Evolution perhaps has not gone far enough along for us to pull our feet clean out of the mire; the wrong in us is a kind of hang-over from our brute ancestry. The only trouble is that the wrong in us is not primitive; it is mature. Life does not grow out of it; life grows into it. I can do far more harm in my world than Machiavelli could do in his. There is progress in righteousness; but there is progress in wickedness to keep step with it. Or we assure you that it has been civilization itself which has separated us from our original innocence; the ignorance of legislators, the tyranny of rulers and priests, the conflict of class, the rise of the machine. Professor Dewey of Columbia thinks it is a faulty educational technique. He may have something there! But nobody will enlighten us, in the phrase of Reinhold Niebuhr,[19] as to how a wrong that doesn't exist in man himself ever got into the order which men have created. And nobody seems thoroughly willing to make up his mind about the way out, whether it lies up or down, forward or back.

Jesus treated evil as a fact. Whatever its origin, its being here admitted of no doubt. He kept saying what only the bitter lessons of history have brought us once more to guess at: that deep in every human life there is somehow that which defiles it. *From within, from the heart of man, the designs of evil come* (Mark 7:21), *the lust of the flesh, and the pride of life,* which are *not of the Father, but of the world* (I John 2:16; A.V.). That is the only soberly realistic view of human nature there is. It always has compelled the minds of men at the last. It always will.

And just there this Christ lays hold of us, not in crowds, but one by one, with constant awe in his eyes, as if nothing mattered but that beggar lying at a rich man's gate—or was it really the rich man at the beggar's gate?—, that woman flung on her knees by the men who wanted to see her die, somebody peering at him from the branches of a sycamore tree, a homesick boy who had trudged off into a far country. Never in all of human history was such a price laid on the human soul, its vast dimension of sin matched only by its still vaster dimension of God.

Quietly he wore for you and me this gift of life like taffeta and ermine, to keep us from having to theorize about it, and imagine, and dream dreams, and suppose that maybe it is great. Look at him and call it cheap if you can. At best any decent estimate of it without him would have been little more than a high-minded sort of guess. What confronts us now is not an estimate but a record. There was a poet once by the name of Homer, so tradition says; and he, or they, as the case may be, wrote poetry. After that people did not have to reckon how great a thing poetry might be; they saw it for themselves and read it. So also there was a philosopher once by the name of Socrates, and here we are on firmer ground historically. He gave philosophy much of its impetus as he went prying about with his candle into the dark recesses of this mysterious being of ours. Since then we have not had to reckon how great a thing philosophy might be; we can go and see for ourselves. By the same token there was a Master once of life. He spoke of it in terms of beauty, reverently; he lived out its immortal destiny for it with clear and lofty grandeur, carrying it unhurt through death; men saw him do it, and wrote it down. Since then nobody has had to suppose, or presume, or hazard the guess that life after all may be a very great thing. It is, or else you have to get rid somehow of this troublesome Galilean. And that you cannot do. What he said and what he did will not let go. It is just there, today and tomorrow, to keep every man's sneer from making sense.

It would hardly seem necessary to point out what release there is in all this, not only from the foolish despair which settles down over us because we think we do not amount to anything, but also from the fitful hopes that every once in a while come so near destroying us because they have no root except in the shallow soil of our own poor lives. It is like losing a broken compass at sea to find the stars again.

The pressure that rests upon us precisely now in history, when human life is at one of its lowest ebbs, is the pressure to give it back that private universe of its own to which it has a right and which it must have if it is going to face the world again with any dignity or any hope, in a universe where the soul is and sin is and the power of God. For this one reason, if for no other, neither a political nor an economic but a religious enterprise alone holds the key to the future. By every discipline at our command, by every truth that is in our keeping, man must be brought to reaffirm his stature as a child of God. Until he does, he is like the shoe-black in *Sartor Resartus*. All the financiers and upholsterers and confectioners joined together in stock-company cannot make him happy. It is the Infinity within him that turns him into a misfit, a square peg in the round hole of this tangible universe, arranges for him to be miserable until he reaches out his hands in the dark to have them caught by the hands of God, teases him and prods him, and refuses to leave him alone.

Let Walt Whitman have his picture of a cow knee-deep in clover chewing her cud as his ideal of peace. If he had ever achieved it, he would not have been Walt Whitman; he would have been a cow. *The foxes have holes,* so Jesus put it, *and the birds of the air have nests; but the Son of man*—and we lose the force of this entirely unless we understand that he meant not only his own but all the restless souls of God's creation—*hath not where to lay his head* (Matthew 8:20; Luke 9:58— A.V.). He is forever less than he would be and always condemned to be more than he seems. Even the winged bulls on the ancient walls of Assyria bear witness to that in him which, though akin to the beast, is poised momentarily for flight.

From that contempt of himself, then, which is the source of his psychopathic insistence on the silly distinctions of class and color and race that never distinguish; from his contempt of others which is the very root of immorality, tossing about this unspeakably precious thing which life is as if it were refuse; from the poverty of every present lot; from his anonymous obscurity: let the pulpit of the twentieth century recall him, joint-heir with Jesus Christ, meet to be a partaker of the inheritance of the saints in light (Romans 8:17; Colossians 1:12—A.V.). The preaching which week after week lends itself to that will not be ineffective preaching.

There is but one central sanctity—a man, with the hand of God upon him. The civilization which loses sight of it blows up and falls apart. The system which refuses to build itself around the incalculable and sovereign worth of human personality is doomed before it gets to its feet. We need no new faith; we need a larger faith. You and I are here to let out what faith we have from the seams that have drawn and disfigured it—until it fits our life again.

### III

And there is but one final vantage point from which we can do it. We are pressed home now directly to the third of those chief heads or accents under which I have said that the sermon, if it is to be whole and central and true, has to move as under banners,—the third of these great *securities of the faith* which are to be kept through all the turmoil of our time *intact* (I Timothy 6:20; II Timothy 1:14),—the third and most indispensable weapon in the apostle's armory. We have been within sight of it all along. It is what Paul calls in the introduction of his letter to the Romans

The Gospel of God Concerning His Son*

There is
no Christian doctrine of God the Father without it. Without
it there is no Christian doctrine of man, the child of God. Not
only is it essential to each; it is the inevitable link between
them. There is a given-ness about God, and there is a given-
ness about man. There is a given-ness, too, about Christ.

The Foundation Is Laid

Paul sets it down
soberly; (I Corinthians 3:11) *namely Jesus Christ, and no one
can lay any other.* To the Galatians he breaks through the bonds
of restraint, passionately: *Even though it were myself or some
angel from heaven, whoever preaches a gospel that contradicts
the gospel I preached to you, God's curse be on him! I have
said it before and I now repeat it: . . . God's curse be on him!*
(1:8, 9)[20] Here we are at the final toss. Christ means that the
pivotal fact of being is not our sin but God's deliverance. He
means that cosmically or he means nothing: not this present
and tangled wrong, but that ultimate and sovereign Right, underneath and through and back of all created things, deeper
than man's inhumanity to man, deeper than pain and death;

The Likeness of the Unseen God

in Whom *the
divine Fulness willed to settle without limit, to reconcile in his
own person all on earth and in heaven alike, in a peace made
by the blood of his cross* (Colossians 1:15, 19, 20).

It is this invasion of Time by Eternity which constitutes the
sole ground of our hope. Perhaps we should lift it here into
high relief. In a very real sense, as we have already seen, the
darkest tragedies of our time have sprung from the efforts we
have made to reverse the process. We have done what we could
with our commando raids to get a foothold on that other shore.

---

* Romans 1:1, 3.

And the project has seemed to us highly religious. We have stared long at nature, trying to put two and two together and arrive at mind. We have stared long at history, trying to make two follow one and lead to three, which is "a power not ourselves that makes for righteousness." We are staring in our new theology at sin, trying to pile Pelion on Ossa, doom on judgments, and arrive at something outside the historical process.

And all of it talks double talk. These are the separate chapters in the story of the man who would be God. The Christian religion is the story of the God Who would be man. We don't come to "the knowledge of certain characteristics as divine" and then discover them in Jesus who, in the words of another, went up and down Palestine revealing "something about God which he had become more clearly acquainted with in his experience" than we have in ours.[21] What we have in Jesus of Nazareth is not what people have thought out. It is not just the account of a chosen few, with what we ourselves have been able to read between the lines. It is what God has done.

We must assume then steadfastly and unavoidably that all preaching worthy of the name is to have its center and focus in Jesus himself, that figure of the past who is our present Lord. The pulpit has been avoiding him long enough. One minister as old as I am told me recently that for a quarter of a century he had been doing it. God seemed to provide material a plenty, and not so confusing. Nor was there in that to his way of thinking any note of vast defection. It is Christ who is the way in which men must walk. It is he who is the word and truth and act of God. He is that life which is eternal. Preaching what he preached, as Denney once pointed out, is not preaching Christianity. This never satisfied Paul. There is amazingly little of that in the epistles. It has never satisfied anybody. Preaching him is Christianity, the Only-begotten, the Mediator, whose mediation cost his death: *manifest in the flesh, vindicated by the*

*Spirit, seen by the angels, preached among the nations, believed
on throughout the world, taken up to glory* (I Timothy 3:16).
                    Never Forget Jesus Christ
                                                    *That is my gospel*
(II Timothy 2:8). It is not enough to preach man's inadequacy
and God's peace: what concerns the New Testament is man's
rebellion and God's redemption, man's desperate loss and God's
desperate hazard. The *glad, good news* (Romans 10:15) is not
*about* Jesus; it *is* Jesus,—who judges life, ransoms life, and sets
life upright on its feet again. It is not a concept; it is a power.
It is not a formula or a dogma or a system, but a presence which
still moves on in the dangerous vanguard of human life; so that
not to obey his word proves strangely like running down a steep
place into the sea. "Yesterday is old," cried George Matheson,
"last year is like a faded garment; but Thou art not old. Thy
years do not fail. Modern as I am, O Son of Man, I have never
caught up with Thee." There is no clearer fact. There is no
greater mystery. Who knows Christ, says Martin Luther, knows
all.

Let me beseech you therefore, wherever you take your text,
make across country, as fast as ever you can, to him! That is
Spurgeon's phrase: unless it becomes our practice we shall be
giving men a stone, when it is bread, only bread, they need!
Usher men into his company. If we fail in that we have failed
indeed and betrayed our trust beyond all hope of remedy. It is
Christ who must "confront the demons"; it is Christ who must
stand "in the midst of the conflict" so that no one can escape
him. Else all your pains have gone for naught, and God's word
is that day, for all you have done, unspoken in the ears of your
congregation. There was not much that was new in Christian
teaching. Christ was new. He was the authentic majesty of God,
authenticated by the very laying of it aside. Where else was God
so vast? The star of Bethlehem was like an asterisk in the text

of history; and this was the footnote at the bottom of the page: *Whoever wants to be great among you must be your servant* (Matthew 20:26). It was not creation that showed God great; it was Jesus, this eternal light on the hearth of our poor earth, this eternal love like the beating of blood behind a sleepless brow: *O Jerusalem, Jerusalem! slaying the prophets and stoning those who have been sent to you! How often I would fain have gathered your children as a fowl gathers her brood under her wings,*—think of God's remembering that from the back yard at Nazareth! *How often! But you would not!* (Matthew 23:37) What was vast was "the fluttering of this veil of silence" which rests over our hurt world: the glory that stirred for a moment at last on two beams of wood, and then grew strangely still again—for little people. That was new.

And with it God pulled out the diapason stop on His mighty organ. The rest would have been but thin music had he not. The rest is thin music now. To say that Christ is central to Christian preaching is to fall so far short of the truth that to say no more would be unrelieved tragedy. The story of the cross is central to the preaching of Christ. (I Corinthians 1:17.) There seems to have come a time in the life of Paul, as there must come a time in ours if what we say is to have power, when words and wisdom were laid aside, and he determined to be ignorant of everything except

Christ the Crucified

*—a stumbling block to the Jews, "sheer folly" to the Gentiles, but for those who are called, whether Jews or Greeks, a Christ who is the power of God and the wisdom of God,* (I Corinthians 1:23, 24; 2:2; Galatians 3:1; 6:14) *in whom* every living soul might find *redemption, even the forgiveness of sins* (Colossians 1:14, A.V.).

I am not particularly concerned with how that works. It is not at all necessary to have a neat, judicial, mathematical theory of the atonement. The fact of it is for any life to handle. We may not define it as closely as our fathers did. It may be for us that not alone the death but the birth and resurrection of our Lord, with all the years between, the whole and living Christ, are involved in this act and assurance of God's pardon and power; but the pardon itself and the power, these are present and gracious realities.

And they stand up not around the circumference but at the center of human experience, because sin stands there: to be met in the gospel with more than love; to be met with rescue. There all that could become man in God and all that could become God in man got into the world to work out His holy will, not around the edges but from the very heart and core of all that is worst and most irrevocable about living. Our century, the death that rains out of the skies, stripped and broken lives wandering forlornly across the frontiers of Europe, war chattering its red insanities on the horizon of every day that dawns, your life, my life, with their old habits that cling like barnacles to the ship's hull, all of it piling up into weird and monstrous shapes! The hand that lays hold of it is terrible, crushing empires; but pierced, bringing life again out of death: lifting all our wrong and our rebellion until it becomes as it were God's own, and He Himself becomes its victim. There is no deliverance out of the process of history. There is deliverance in it, and that by a God who is "not alone outside it or against it," but in the process Himself.

Let it be set down here that no theology which unlike the New Testament bogs down in the doctrine of sin is going to be of much service to us in the recovery of that classic message. It is still essentially a message of salvation. It spoke through Hebrew prophecy. Such realism as is ours today in the realm of retributive righteousness would have proved itself no Lord's song in a strange land there by the waters of Babylon. Already it was balanced by a realism in the realm of unmerited grace which became on the lips of a little band of Galilean fishermen a shout of accomplished victory. There is a salvation, not eschatological but mundane; there is a coming of truth and mercy and justice in history which no man can work, but which every man is yet under bond to receive as the free gift in Christ of a gracious and mighty God.

This it was that happened at Calvary. Not in Bethlehem, not in Nazareth, but on Golgotha. The cross is not a symbol; it is an act. It is God's conquering presence in the world that he made. If we should conspire against it and refuse to mention it any more for a century or so, life would still come back to it, sure that something was missing, rediscover it, and sit down in its shadow again oddly at home.

I wonder if you have ever noticed how all the "great, sad literature of the soul" does just that. In Shakespeare, for instance, how straight and unerring the movement is! When he began to write,[22] he wrote comedy, facile, tender comedy, drawing men with such sympathy that you cannot help adoring them, even that fat, swashbuckling liar, Falstaff, set on his huge legs so kindly to carry his stomach about! But then something happened. Shakespeare threw Falstaff away, had to be rid of him. If such a fellow could conquer the world, the world was not worth conquering. There were bare, rude heights of human life, mysterious, dark caverns that had to be explored; and it was painful business. It is for all of us. For a while the great poet's sympathy seems to have turned sour, his gentleness into a passion of contempt. He acts as if he wants to lash out at humanity and wither it. If I were God,—did not Luther say so once of the world?—I should kick it to pieces! Shakespeare writes as if he were nauseated by it, trying to fling it from him like filth, putting his heel on it as you do on an insect that drags its slime over God's green earth. Then little by little it dawns on him: the way to supreme happiness is by love, and that love moves forward inevitably to awe-inspiring tragedy. There is no scorn in Macbeth, no sneer, nothing so cheap or shallow as disdain. You stand in the thane's shoes, live poignant hours with him, feel the fierce fires kindling so weirdly in his soul; until, except for the fires that still rage, it turns black, and the flame leaps and sears its horrible red will, and life comes crackling and tumbling down in appalling ruin, as if on your own head. But there is something like the pity of God in it, and in Hamlet, and in Othello, and in Lear: something very like the shadow of a cross!

So in the history of human life has Calvary seemed like the last word of all, against sin and wrong and evil speaking: God's word, and not another's, saying itself across the gulf, through all the dumb red horror on "the world's great altar stairs," beyond speech into deed, never to be forgotten, never! It is not anyone's failure. It is not the giving up of anything, not even of life. It is the achievement of something. Not a fate heroically endured, but a mission deliberately undertaken. A task finished. The issue of it, far from being tragic, is a shout! Christ does not sink into death. He mounts into it, and reaches out his hand for a sceptre. He is not being blown about like a scrap of paper by the winds of circumstance, and caught fast on a gallows: he is changing the whole face of the earth. This is no dismal rout; it is an incredible conquest. *He cancelled the regulations that stood against us,* listen to Paul,—*all these obligations he set aside when he nailed them to the cross, when he cut away the angelic Rulers and Powers from us, exposing them to all the world and* Triumphing Over Them*

It is God's *yes* to life's *no*. It is His tortured knowledge, standing for a moment on the brink, then making its reckless plunge to get to the bot-

* Colossians 2:14, 15.

tom of the farthest estate to which a man can fall, just as the
eagle is said to dart with the swiftness of the wind to spread her
wings under one of her fledglings as it drops. It is a love that
has taken to shattering all that is so terribly wrong in the world,
as the cross itself was shattered, while it gathers into its arms the
huge pathos of a ruined creation, not to change the past so
much as to change the future.

You see Him quietly putting aside the wine mingled with
myrrh. He will not be drugged. This deep transaction shall not
slip by in a haze. Not for a moment will he loosen his hold
on it, writes Dr. Gossip.

>           —to feel the fog in my throat,
>   The mist in my face, . . .
> I would hate that death bandaged my eyes, and forbore,
>   And bade me creep past.
> No! let me taste the whole of it . . .[23]

Once only he cries out against the desolate thing: *My God, my
God, why hast thou forsaken me?* (Matthew 27:46; Mark 15:
34) But read that psalm. It is the twenty-second. I hardly see
how he could have failed to think of it. They even mocked and
tossed their heads and sneered at him in its very words.[24] *He
left it to the Eternal! Let Him come to the rescue if He cares
for him!* So Jesus began to quote it. Surely he meant more than
this first verse. Read it as it turns back confidently to the long
past of Israel, like a ship that has suddenly careened to her gun-
wales under the sharp blast of some hurricane, only to right herself, water pouring in great floods from her bow. In Egypt it
was, when night had fallen, and the waters of the Red Sea
lapped at their feet, while the rumble of Pharaoh's chariots was
like low thunder on the horizon. *On thee our fathers did rely,
and thou didst rescue them.* There were the long yesterdays
sweeping in. God was not one kind of God then and another
kind of God now. Read on as the psalm catches up with the

childhood of the psalmist: *'Twas thou indeed didst take me from the womb, didst lay me on my mother's breast.* And on, as it looks forward shading its eyes to catch the distant sky-line of the future: *Men shall bethink them of the Eternal, and turn to him from earth's very verge; for the Eternal reigns; his saving deeds shall be declared to generations yet unborn.* That is not bewilderment and despair: that is hope and faith and love working their steady way through the dark, and coming at last to this: *Father, I trust my spirit to thy hands* (Luke 23:46). Under Bethlehem one writes the words: *Sic Deus Amavit.* Under Calvary: *Sic Regnat Deus!*

We always have to start and stop with this mysterious note of triumph if we want to understand the cross or come anywhere within a long sea-mile of it. I remember seeing Judith Anderson as Mary in that moving play, *Family Portrait.*[25] With the pent-up agony of a mother's heart, she wondered at this cruel thing they had done to him, to her peace-loving, kindly, eldest son. She could see no sense in it at all. But the hours passed, and a child was born there in Nazareth to her youngest son Judah. Shyly she came to him when she heard; fooled with her apron for a moment; then asked him, smiling a little wanly, to call the child Jesus. "Because," she explained, "because I would not have him to be forgotten!" She need not have worried. As she lights a candle and turns away to the window, you hear the music of a hymn, and the lengthening shadow of the Crucified falls over all the earth.

The simple fact is that the cross never stayed on the hill where they put it. It marched out across the Roman Empire. It leaped on those proud standards and got itself emblazoned there. It fluttered over Europe, in dark forests, on lonely castles. And began to point the patient centuries to a better way of treating men than man had found. It brought them face to face with the stark reality of love's triumph where hate would

always fail. Very few believed it really, but multitudes halt-
ingly swore devotion to it. They betrayed it and denied it, but
they took off their helmets and knelt before it. They slew
and slandered, tortured and hated; but it towered over their
heads as they looked up to it, and they made the sign of it on
their breasts. It was such a hard way to follow; but they knew
in their hearts that there was no other. It was God's eternal
business in this world. The sun set on Calvary as it has set
all the days, but men were not rid of Jesus.

Why? None of what has followed through the ages, for all its
sublimity, would have been intelligible had there not been another conclusion different from that of *Family Portrait,* implicit
in every chapter of the story. It grows on you as you move along
through the record. Try some time leaving out the sequel. As I
went home from the theatre that night, something I had remembered kept ringing through my head. *If in this life we have
nothing but a mere hope in Christ, we are of all men to be pitied
most. But it is not so!*

### Christ Did Rise*

Whatever it was that
happened—and I suppose the details of it will never be clear;
though the apostles will tell you with one voice of the fact—it
was the impulse which started the Christian Church on its
splendid march through the centuries, splendid both in tragedy
and in triumph. If it had been fiction, it would hardly have
held up in a world fiercer even in some ways than ours, with
nothing to support it but the "nonsense" of a little company of
men and women who had scrambled to their feet against an
empire. For them, at least, there had dawned a day which was
God's vindication of His order, when He had redeemed His
pledge of victory. The resurrection to them was His way of intimating that you could not finish off the Sermon on the Mount

* I Corinthians 15:19, 20; also verses 1–9.

with a grin and a hammer in your hand. I am told now that it is abrogated for the duration. People have said *No* to it before and God has said *Yes.* You could not bring Jesus of Nazareth to a dead-letter office, or the life he shared with us. It was not a tale told by an idiot,—they were sure of it,—full of sound and fury, signifying nothing.[26] It had its stated origins, it had its orderly processes, and it had its appointed issues. It was intent on something else besides just "dying off at the top." It was not only moving; it was going somewhere. And nails could not stop it. And a grave could not stop it. The very integrity of the universe was at stake, really. Creation could not be made to look ridiculous. It had not been wound up to run down into nothing but the skull of poor Yorick,[27] as if that could be the catchall of poor Yorick's hopes and fears and the end-all of poor Yorick's existence.

And so, *very early on the first day of the week* (Mark 16:2), the story of redemption was put out in its final form. Pilate and that Good Friday crowd had tried to edit it. *Blessed are the humble;* and alongside now this contradiction stood: *He went away carrying the cross* (Matthew 5 and John 19:17). *Blessed are the merciful,—to the spot called the "place of the skull." Blessed are the poor in heart,—there they crucified him.* But the Author of all things drew a line through the contradictions and wrote across the original text with His own hand, *Stet,* let it stand. Let it all stand, forever. *They saw a youth sitting on the right dressed in a white robe. You are looking for Jesus of Nazareth? He has risen, he is not here* (Mark 16:5, 6).

That is why the cross to this very hour speaks no uncertain language. The central problem of the Christian religion is still the solemn and continuing demand it lays on us. It offers no argument. It gives no reason. It makes no exception. It means that every way but God's way is specious and not real. He chose the cross because nothing else would do. And He had everything else. He had more knowledge than we will ever scrape together. He had more power than the United Nations could generate if they were rotating round the Axis. And none of it was enough. He chose to stake the future on those two beams of wood. That was His wisdom. That was His power. It is not likely that you and I can skirt around the edges of it coyly. *In hoc signo vinces!* It is woven into the pattern by the hand that did the weaving.

Things are so hopeless with us, not because the cross will not work any more, if I may put it so crudely, but because nothing else will. It plagues us with tasks that are too big for us, with mad, heroic things, "preposterous, wild imaginings." Not for a moment is it over, and not for a moment does it mean that we have to put up with wrongs. Jesus did not come all the way down to this earth for that. It does mean, besides all the rest, that we are here to cancel the wrongs and to redeem the people who do them. Not to suffer something, but to accomplish something! Not to endure, but to conquer! There is no need anywhere of the merely passive virtues that organize themselves all too often into impotence and call themselves a church. There is need only of those who, with that sound from heaven once more in their ears, *like a violent blast of wind* (Acts 2:2), will carry a load on their backs and life in both hands, not without scars.

It is not pity Christ wants. He wants creation by the living might of His spirit to get into chaos, and He has shown us how: here in the unending heartache of God, from which nobody can go home and get out his slippers and sit comfortably by the fire. There is more than pardon in the touch of it. It keeps haunting us all with the suggestion of undiscovered possibilities, as if we had never really seen or understood this ineffably great thing, whispering forever that you, being yourself but a poor object of God's grace, are nevertheless one other hope He has for His world. And you turn toward the road that leads from an empty grave, on a pilgrimage most sure, in the wake of multitudes that no man can number, marked with His sign, men and women who somehow have learned to "go gaily in the dark."

Here is one of them. He is a sailor, and he is writing a letter. It is a letter about a young woman who is a member of my congregation. He is writing it to her employer.

Dear Sir:

I'm a sailor and I'll be pulling out in a few hours but first I've got something I want to say. I came into your office this morning lonely and scared to death about sailing again. . . . I wanted to talk to somebody pretty bad. So when the girl at the desk said hello I went in and asked her if she had a job for me. She said for me to sit down for a few minutes so I did. . . . I told her maybe there wouldn't be jobs or anything afterwards, that if a fellow could only be sure something would come through, worth dying for, it wouldn't be so bad. She smiled (she's got a friendly kind of smile) and said that's easy. Christ is coming through and He's worth dying for. I just looked at her and she talked as if He was alive and a good pal of hers. I sort of expected to see Him walk in the door, it was so real.

I was only there about ten minutes and I don't know why but her talking like that sort of did something to me, and I'm not lonely any more and I'm not scared. It was like she had said, I want to make you acquainted with my friend Jesus. You ought to get to know each other since he'll be going your way. I'm 19 and I never knew before that there was a God like that who would go along with a fellow. It don't matter so much now if my ship goes down and I go down as long as there's a God that no sub can sink and that won't ever change from what's right even if the war goes on forever!

I wanted to tell that girl thank you but I didn't want her to think of me as fresh. Maybe you could tell her for me—and thank you.

Respectfully and gratefully yours,

&ᘛ ᘚᕽ

Up! mind thine own aim, and
God speed the mark!

RALPH WALDO EMERSON

ⲁⲁⲁⲁⲁⲁⲁⲁⲁⲁⲁⲁⲁⲁⲁⲁⲁⲁⲁⲁⲁⲁⲁⲁⲁⲁⲁⲁⲁⲁⲁⲁⲁⲁⲁⲁⲁⲁ

# Chapter 4

## GOD APPEALING BY ME

ⲁⲁⲁⲁⲁⲁⲁⲁⲁⲁⲁⲁⲁⲁⲁⲁⲁⲁⲁⲁⲁⲁⲁⲁⲁⲁⲁⲁⲁⲁⲁⲁⲁⲁⲁⲁⲁⲁ

It is then the given-ness of God, the given-ness of Man, and the
given-ness of Christ down the years of human history, these
*securities of the faith* (I Timothy 6:20), which constitute the
essential challenge and perpetual succor of the Christian gospel:
challenge because it comes to us as probe and judgment, as
claim and demand; succor because it comes with comfort and
healing, as redemption and promise. But it comes; we are not
its proprietors; we are its stewards. *I am an envoy for Christ,*
writes the apostle; *God appealing by me, as it were* (II Corinthians 5:20). *I tell you,* he goes on in another place, *the gospel is*
Not a Human Affair*

The weapons of his
warfare are divinely strong because they were not forged in any
human armory! And, on the instant, be brings us face to face

* Galatians 1:11.

with the first question I want to raise here. It is the question that was put to Jesus: By what authority doest thou these things? And who gave thee this authority? (Matthew 21:23, A.V.) With what claim and title that can be announced and vindicated can a man enter the pulpit of a Christian church? Surely he must come with a larger warrant than can be mustered for his own opinion. *For we preach not ourselves* (II Corinthians 4:5 A.V.).

Suppose we say right away that in all such fiercely critical moods as ours the answer is not one thing, to be allowed or disallowed. It is a number of things. Certainly what warrant we have resides first of all in the actuality of divine revelation. We in our turn, as were the Jews, have been *entrusted with the scriptures of God* (Romans 3:2). This revelation is to be considered not merely as an incident; but as a process that breaks in at Bethlehem upon all incidents, cuts across them at Calvary, and transcends them in the resurrection; complete, but not final; itself a Person, yet recorded in a book; within time but of eternity; not what men have said or written or felt about the redeeming act of God, so much as that act itself which is His Word. There need be little desire to insist on any mechanical doctrine of inspiration. There need be no tendency at all to hide from the results of reverent and critical scholarship. But neither on that account need there be any very great perplexity. I do not find myself even wanting the rigidity of copy-book authority. God's living Word could not be reduced to such terms, however passionate my wish. His self-revelation has taken place within the limits of history. The record of that divine initiative is a historical document. But the revelation itself, by which God continues to present Himself as an object of knowledge to the minds of men, cannot be circumscribed within and made subject to the historical process. *No man,* says Paul, *no man put it into my hands* (Galatians 1:12). No more did any man put it into ours. It is not so simple as that. As Richard Niebuhr has pointed out, the history set down is caught up and interpreted by the revelation; and we ourselves are a part of that history. The Bible is not a literature "created by the people of God." It is the disclosure through them to us of the absolute and the eternal.

Perhaps this is why the Bible is its own best credential. There is that about it which bears most potent witness to itself. One finds an amazing difficulty in trying to make these pages speak as if they had come solely from the hearts of men. Yet that, too, is where they came from; and if God has not forgotten how to write, such pages as are still to be written must come from ours. So do we arrive at the fact of experience. When the talk is of authority, there is such a thing as the free response of a man's own faith to the felt presence and power of the Almighty. And it cannot be dismissed with a wave of the hand!

## My Little Boast

Paul calls it, and sets down the proud story of his life, *with all my labours, with all my lashes, with all my time in prison* (II Corinthians 11:16, 23). What he had was his now, words like nails driven home! Say what you will, the question ultimately becomes not Is the Bible so? but Is the Bible so for me? Our part in the transaction is not final in the sense that there is nothing beyond; but neither is it ridiculous.

"In the end the individual must walk by his own insight."[1] One thing is sure; we can beat no sullen retreat nowadays in the direction of a stubborn and unabashed dogmatism, whether it be of the Bible or of the church; covering it as best we can with a rear guard of apologetics, all too often incompetent, irrelevant, and unnecessary. There is no call to desert or browbeat the human in our effort to confront it with the divine. The primary stock in trade of the early church was "witnessing," the quiet testimony of men who had discovered for themselves the only practical value which truth has: its capacity for translating itself again into life, distilling under God out of revelation into experience, and out of experience into revelation again, without waste and without loss.

Herein lies the weakness of both modernism and fundamentalism. Modernism oriented itself around an attempt to discover in reason the seat and source of the only unchallenged authority that is available, trimming the sails of Christianity to *every passing wind* of science, and giving itself to the task of domesticating the Kingdom of God, for privileged Protestants at least, within the profound but unperceived coercions and brutalities of human nature; while fundamentalism, valid in its reaction but without discernment, and therefore equally *dexterous in devising error* (Ephesians 4:14), attempted to orient itself around a cautious slavery to the letter, making men "deaf to the music of heaven," and stopping the great soul of the Bible dead in its tracks, stiffened into a kind of *rigor mortis.*

One can only be devoutly grateful for the new attitude which in our day has begun to shape itself with regard to the historic faith of the Christian church. Occasionally you will find it heralded in the candles and liturgies with which some would now fain cover their uncertainty with regard to the Apostles' Creed and the Ten Commandments, putting on another stole every time the conscience grows uneasy, and singing another chant for every article of Westminster or Augsburg that has slipped out of their worship! One is reminded of that devastating statement of the humanists' doctrine: 'There is no God, and the Virgin Mary is His mother! Here is nothing but Virgil's Cyclops rolling over in his sleep. It is of no concern. What thrills me is that there is a stirring of Atlas in our times!

The only trouble is that crisis now fills our sky. Judgment seems to be as yet the only word theologians can spell. Of grace and immanence they still know little. Sin is written in huge letters across their mind; redemption and the saving might of God they fear as they fear the devil of liberalism. Justification is the apple of their eye; sanctification is their blind spot. History is the place of relativity and despair, with the cross of Christ at the edge of it: precisely the same sort of rebuttal that the Book of Enoch offered to the visionary and romantic Psalms of Solomon in those centuries that intervened between the Old Testament and the New; and both of them were wrong. And both of them were right! When I am told by this new school that progress is out, except for certain "impossible possibilities," I find myself struggling with a language which is neither Hebrew nor Greek, in which I daresay even God Himself may have some difficulty! When I am told that even social service is a "biting on granite," not only language but morality ceases to have any meaning.

Yet surely this way and not another lies the future. It is no return to medievalism. It is a plain coming to our senses; and by way of bitter experience and travail of soul. We are finding out that it is not a slope up, called evolution, that we are facing. We are not living in a world which is being lifted inch by inch out of its poor estate. We are living in a world where there is something that is incorrigible; so vast and demonic that God Himself had to get into it and die before anything could be done about it; until out of despair is born not cynicism, but courage. Not defeat, or absolute conflict, or paradox, so much as tension. Not idealism; realism—which is idealism in the process of becoming incarnate on my street: a gallant facing of the dark with a faith that is not subservient to facts, but creates them. *Credo in unum Deum, Patrem Omnipotentem.*

What warrant we have then runs back to a book; it bears on it the witness of our own experience; and it carries written across the back what Paul calls in the Second Epistle to the Corinthians (1:19)

## The Divine "Yes" in Christ

The surest claim we have comes from a Person, whose very presence it is that keeps his will alive. Against him men do not revolt; against him men break and destroy themselves. What he says, life repeats and at the last enforces. But every soul must make its own choice, standing on its feet with the eyes of God upon it *in the face of Jesus Christ* (II Corinthians 4:6, A.V.). Beyond that there is no other court of appeal. Nothing in the end is more peremptory. And nothing in the end is more desperately perilous.

Do you remember how Ivan, the most intellectual member of that weird trio of *The Brothers Karamazov,* tells of the poem he has written and called The Grand Inquisitor? The scene is laid in Seville the day after the burning of hundreds of heretics in one of those bloody carnivals which made the sixteenth century so lurid. Christ had come to visit his people. The tortured folk flocked to him. He healed the blind. A little seven-year-old girl was borne in her white coffin down the steps of the cathedral. Softly he whispered to her, *"Talitha cumi";* and answering she rose and looked wonderingly about. With a frown the Grand Inquisitor stood watching, not now clad in his gorgeous pontificals as he had been yesterday, but wearing only in ostentatious humility an old monk's cassock. Suddenly and sternly he pointed to Jesus, and to the guard that followed him snapped out an order, "Arrest that man!" Hours later he stole into the dungeon with his lantern. Its light flickered wanly on the walls, while he upbraided his prisoner bitterly for coming to earth again and upsetting what little human authority the church had been able to patch together against that unmanageable freedom which had come out of Nazareth. His eyes seemed to burn through the darkness with fanatic fire. On and on poured the tumult of his speech, until it spent itself in the threat and sentence of death. And Christ spoke never a word. Quietly in the silence that fell he drew near and kissed the old man on his bloodless lips. That was the whole answer. And those lips began to tremble. The eyes that burned with fire slowly widened. The Grand Inquisitor stumbled backward, then turned blindly to the door. He threw it open and screamed, "Go and come no more. Come not at all, never, never!" And Jesus went out into the dark streets of the town. One sees the peril of it; but there is no escape. The only final authority in life is the defenseless authority of an eternal presence—playing his part indeed, as Nels Ferré has said, "in the push of the imperfect forces of human history, while at the same time he stands continually before it with the pull of his perfect purpose."[2]

Today around that mind and that purpose entwine all the victories and defeats of twenty centuries in the unity of the Christian church, which is as much a part of the given-ness of God as Christ is: the work of no man, of no group of men, but the work of the Holy Spirit to the glory of God and to our salvation; holy, catholic, and apostolic. Here, too, is God's act in history, and God's word, *Who called you to*

This Fellowship with His Son

*Jesus Christ our Lord* (I Corinthians 1:9). Here is more than the "lengthened shadow of a man"; here is the Word still incarnate of the Holy Ghost, made flesh to dwell among us. And to that living, organic body, past, present, and future, are we bound; being *severally members one of the other.* (Romans 12:5; I Corinthians 12:12–27)

To its own continuing hurt, Protestant Christianity never yet has elaborated any adequate doctrine of the Christian church; nor has it any adequate realization of its oneness. Surely this is that sinew which the angel touched in his wrestling. *And Jacob called the name of the place Peniel: for I have seen God face to face.... And as he passed over ... the sun rose upon him, and he halted upon his thigh.* (Genesis 32:30, 31, A. V.) Out of the Reformation came not a community, but a passion for individualism, an obsession with freedom; and therein, for all the shining of our sun, do we now halt! To be a Protestant once meant to be a witness *for* something, *pro testis;* it is now coming to mean one who is constitutionally given over to raising objections. Perhaps, under the pressure of hard necessity, freed somewhat of our weird addiction to palliatives, we shall discover again our original genius for confession, and in the process rally our scattered forces. If not by the organic union of the churches, then by the growth within them of a deep sense of that God-imposed unity which is presently ours in Christ with all who truly confess his blessed name as Saviour and Lord. By no moving about on the surface of things, writes Berdyaev, by no sacrifice of variety to uniformity, by no tolerance which in itself is subversive of faith, but by an earnest pressing in along the lines of mutual recognition to the heart and center of the Christian gospel. Not for four hundred years have the horizons been so bright with the promise of it.

Meanwhile, it is out of that fellowship which is the strong and living witness of the redeemed that we must come to speak, if we are to be indeed "the tongue of God's Spirit and the arm of His strength." It is not alone your experience or mine; it is not alone our faith in the eternal Word of God, however firm; it is not alone the divine urgency of Jesus of Nazareth, setting his seal on the human soul. It is the whole Christian church on earth and in heaven, past, present, and to come, the wisdom of the ages, itself part of the saving act of God, which finds its voice through you in the Christian pulpit: here an "island company," as Thomas Hardy somewhere has it,

Standing up fingered, with 'Hark! hark!
The glorious distant sea!'

*Therefore, with angels and archangels, and with all the company of Heaven, we laud and magnify Thy glorious name.*

With this claim, then, and this title we thrust our way across the threshold of the modern world; opposing to its melancholy temper our own deep sense of its tragic need; setting against the panic of all its hurried nostrums the quiet authority of a strangely persistent Word, recorded and incarnate, transcending history and reason and experience, yet at home in them, culminating in the eternal presence and person of Jesus, whose dwelling is still within the Yea and Amen of those that have believed, a multitude *of one heart and of one soul.*

## II

But to whom now does the gospel come? That message which is ours, yet not our own? *God appealing by me,* but to what end?

Certainly this saving Word comes first to the individual. *There is*

### A New Creation

*whenever a man comes to be in Christ* (II Corinthians 5:17). Here is its primary and inevitable function: not to anybody apart from others, but to everybody alone, in and through the relationships which he inevitably bears. Surely there can no longer be any question of that.

There is a certain stealth about the Word of God. The things that take place on the surface of life, catch your eye in the headlines, deafen your ears on the street, prove so often to be of such little moment. It is all a boisterous, raucous hullabaloo on top. Underneath is the subtle, silent, decisive drift.

You read the story of the Roman Empire during the reigns of Augustus and the gloomy Tiberius. Armies are tramping north through the forests of Germany. Magnificent marble buildings are springing up in Rome. You get a fleeting glimpse of Virgil and Juvenal and Horace in the crowd. Strange temples appear, with their stranger priests from Egypt and Persia. You think you catch the dim shape of the world that is to be; but a man is sitting by a well over in Palestine talking to a woman. It is not Caesar that counts, or Pilot, or Herod, but a publican named Matthew collecting the taxes. Not Annas or Caiphas, but a fisherman terrified by a servant girl. And Luke, feeling the hot forehead of this little Jew named Paul. They queer everything.

Or you come on down through fourteen centuries. Once more you think you know how things are moving. In Europe the Roman Church sits splendidly brooding over her vast domain, Patron of Art and Letters. Such a glory of the mind, of brush and chisel, men had not seen before. Over the seas, around the Cape of Good Hope, into the West, her children push out the horizons of her restless life; and in a German village, of a German minister's wife, a child was born. His name was Martin Luther.

That is how human destiny is always shaped; not by blind and relentless forces, meaningless incidents following one another in a meaningless succession through a meaningless panorama of events, but by the God who ever and again takes hold of a human soul and sends it out against "some monstrous wrong," while

> From the cloudy ramparts
> A thousand evil faces jibe and jeer. . . .
>
> But by and by Earth shakes herself, impatiently,
> And down in one great roar of ruin crash,
> Watchtower, and citadel and battlements.

When the red dust has cleared, the lonely soldier
Stands with strange thoughts beneath the friendly stars.[8]

Writes Kagawa in his "Songs from the Slums":

> I cánnot invent
> New things
> Like the airships
> Which sail
> On silver wings;
> But today
> A wonderful thought
> In the dawn was given
> And the stripes on my robe
> Shining from wear
> Were suddenly fair
> Bright with the light
> Falling from Heaven—
> Gold, and silver, and bronze
> Lights from the windows of Heaven.
> And the thought
> Was this:
> That a secret plan
> Is hid in my hand;
> That my hand is big,
> Big,
> Because of this plan;
> That God
> Who dwells in my hand
> Knows this secret plan
> Of the things He will do for the world
> Using my hand!

I do not know how else God works than through the so-called "individualism" of the gospel. The sweep of revelation in history is not from it but toward it. Here is the polestar of our voyage; and none of us may come to salute our captain, reporting with the novice on the old sailing vessel, "Sir, I have passed that star; give me another!" One may have little sympathy with the religion which in so many of our hymns, for instance, to say nothing of our churches, turns out to be an end in itself, taking its satisfactions wherever it can find them, and looking on an evil order with complacency or resignation. But one can have equally little sympathy with a religion which is blindly determined to start with the transformation of human society, breaking one egg after another, as Gerald Heard has it, in the effort to provide that ultimate omelet which we hope sometime to enjoy.

In Jesus' day the air was full of political, social, economic, ecclesiastical, international questions. There were slavery and tyranny and war and intemperance. Two-thirds of the world were slaves, if you like figures, three-quarters drunkards, and nine-tenths adulterers. So it is reported. Yet there is not a word from Jesus' lips that has not to do with human hearts. There for him was the center that fixed the circle. And it must be the center for us.

I have no enthusiasm for any attempt to clean up my street by first hanging pictures on the walls of every apartment and repairing the wash basins, though all this may have to be done. I am saving my first enthusiasm—not so much in point of time as in point of importance—for the attempt to go straight to the middle of things and change men and women; after which both the art and the plumbing presumably will come in for some improvement. It was Lyman Abbott who once said, "You social workers are perfectly lovely to everybody except Christ; and you cut him dead!"[4] Heaven is not a place where everybody belongs to the W.C.T.U. and The Lord's Day Alliance. In Mrs. Browning's homely phrase, "We are not seeking to move humanity to a cleaner stye." Bread-lines and community centers and blue laws, systems, reforms, the alphabetical mysteries of modern government,—these are all poor makeshifts. Yet we keep prating about a social gospel. There is no such thing. There is a gospel with social implications.

The Legislature of Tennessee some years ago in the famous Scopes case issued a formal proclamation disconnecting us from our apelike ancestry. We would better spend our time trying to eradicate certain persistent simian traits from the human bloodstream. It is zoölogical folly going about to salve the bleeding sores of life, which are the lost souls of men, by mixing up and rubbing on the affected parts a highly perfumed passion for the thirty-hour-week! Policies and programs are not of the same order as salvation: they are quite capable of turning out to be its contradictions. They are the issue of redemption; they are not the road to it. They are the feet of religion; but when religion is carried out feet first, it is dead. There is forever something inside that has to happen, lest there be either no desire or the wrong motive or method. We have to come to grips with God by way of "personal encounter;" even as we come to grips with the world. Then shall we hold in our hands a redeeming, transforming power.

I have in my possession the intimate story of a troubled soul who lived out in his own mid-western town the tragic emptiness of those years from 1920 to 1940.

"A brilliant liberal," he wrote, "came to our pulpit. He was so versatile that he attracted many of the irreligious. He gave himself unselfishly and without stint. He was daring, dramatic, militant, at the risk of bitter criticism. His watchword was, 'Life lived in scorn of consequences.' He judged the efficacy of his sermons by the number of listeners who came to him afterwards, saying, 'I believe you will understand my problem and can help me.' His schedule was crowded by a procession of personal interviews with folk representing a wide range of ages, races, and faiths. By the therapy of a Protestant Confessional he demonstrated an amazing capacity for analyzing prob-

lems and describing behavior patterns. Soon he was loved as a
leader of acute spiritual sensitivity and insight. He was quickly
respected as a preacher of integrity and power. He stood for
Christian socialism and was charged with hurting the banks
and other business. He opposed all war and was called a cow-
ard. He favored free speech, providing a meeting place in the
parsonage for radicals who had been excluded from the public
auditorium, and was labeled a communist. He put internation-
alism above nationalism and, of course, must therefore be a
traitor. I heard a labor leader privately tell him, 'You have done
more for the underprivileged in the five years you have been
here than I have been able to accomplish in a lifetime.'

"But the personal gospel was overshadowed by the social.
He seemed unable to integrate the two. A high-school student
unwittingly epitomized our dilemma when almost disgustedly
he exclaimed, 'This church is always facing either a crisis or a
challenge.' Was the transition through which we were passing
the twilight before a dark night or the early dawn of a new
and better day? One question prodded its way into the center
of attention when committees met to plan a program: What is
wrong with what we have? Those primarily interested in
church attendance worried over emptying pews. Some told our
preacher that he was speaking so often in the community that
many did not need to come to church to hear him; others, that
he was leaving the parish so often to speak in distant places that
our local work suffered. But these absences were eloquently ra-
tionalized: Someone had to carry the social gospel to Garcia.
And so it went, through declining morale, with young people
refusing to be 'graduated into a morgue,' worship disintegrat-
ing, study neglected, an indifference that 'could not be sparked
into reality, spontaneity, and growth.' Attempts were made
without success to integrate the work by the revival of the
prayer meeting. But the darkness kept closing in. There was a

mid-week class in psychology and religion. There were forums and lectures on current events, book reviews, music, athletics, and hobbies. But there was also the dark."

And there always will be, as long as there are superficial optimists in our pulpits, however devoted and able, who go all out for building a new world first, and having somewhat to do privately with Jesus of Nazareth a little later. Move over with all your baggage in that direction, and you are due one or two very disturbing realizations. You are due to discover that sin has a certain depth and persistence, not to be uprooted by any genial program for the improvement of general conditions. You are due to discover that the ideals of Jesus always were unattainable and always will be on this earth, else this religion of ours would lose its hold on us by being brought down to the level of the possible. You are due to discover that progress is not inevitable; that even the sacred cow of the nineteenth century, evolution, takes time and is subject to many reverses! Life will not be got at in any such fashion by enthusiasts who are hopeful that by next Wednesday week they will have made all struggle unnecessary by setting us down neatly and precisely at the exact center of the Kingdom of God.

What we need is not a society of justice and righteousness; that perhaps we shall never have. We need individual men and women redeemed, but redeemed into a commonwealth of the redeemed, who will give themselves to the never-ending task of building such a society out of the ruin of our time and every time. They know quite well that they have failed, with all this recalcitrant stuff on their hands. They will never paint the perfect picture or carve the perfect statue. Yet will they strive toward it, as what artist would not? Beaten back, now coming nearer, now falling farther short it may be than ever before; but always in what another has called "the anguish of obedience," —their eyes caught and held by what they have seen of God in the silence, and of His untried will and unfathomed love! History is turned out of its channel, the world is swung on its hinges, not so much by people who have both feet on the ground as by people who have "one foot in heaven"!

There is the premise from which alone this gospel of Jesus Christ can begin to operate socially. That it must is obvious: not only in view of the bitter reproaches leveled at the church for her habitual otherworldliness, and—in spite of her enlightened ideas and progressive sentiments—her practical indifference to the actual conditions in this world which stultify the very news she brings; but most of all because of that universal sense of frustration which has attached itself as one of the outstanding characteristics of our generation to man's age-old quest for community. It is no good any longer forgetting that the essential worth and being of these thousands upon thousands who stand one by one at the focus of the Christian gospel are betrayed and cancelled over and over again by the very complexities and inequities of the society within which, by no choice of their own, they are called on to live. Back in the days of Oliver Cromwell there was a man whose name was Praise-God Barebones. He had a brother with a longer name, Christ-Came-Into-the-World-to-Save Barebones. But still more is behind. There was a third brother, If-Christ-Had-Not-Died-for-Thee-Thou-Hadst-Been-Damned Barebones: which, says Howard Robinson of Oberlin, was just too much name; so they called him Damned Barebones for short. It is all well enough to remember that the Christian gospel is for *you;* but it does not even know you apart from the complexities of this human situation where God has set you to live your life. The order of which we are a part is our business, not primarily perhaps as churchmen, but passionately as Christians. And it is the providential business today of the Christian pulpit. "Stake all on it," says E. Stanley Jones, "and as far as religion is concerned you will have a corpse on your hands; stay out of it and you will have on your hands a ghost." "A church which has only a message is a propaganda institute. A church which has only an altar is an egotistical pursuit of salvation."[5]

In the critical hours when civilizations begin to disintegrate, this last seems to be our peculiar peril. We seek to find refuge in a design for living apart from life, entertaining "the most excellent reasons for shirking our duty." Ministers begin to conceive of themselves again

as spiritual rather than as social or political leaders; to plead a wholesome ignorance of economic and racial realities, some knowledge of which might enable them to deal concretely with the ethical problems of the day; to regard themselves as entrusted with the task of inspiring the people of their churches to do good, rather than with the task of constraining people in the name of God to choose between the concrete goods and evils confronting them.[6]

The Christian gospel becomes a mere wraith of God's purpose, wandering absent-mindedly from room to room of humanity's tragic house, wringing its hands, mumbling its creeds, its best wishes and kindest regards, making its distant gestures toward eternity; not even meeting man's condition, much less shaping anything; apologizing for his poverty; fawning on his governments at war; stroking a cross, but never getting itself crucified because it is not worth crucifying.

Of course, as preachers, we are not expert in any of these matters—politics, sociology, or economics. It would be well to bear that in mind. Modesty should keep us from presumption if nothing else does. Courage becomes a prophet; but so does enough information to make him quite sure that he knows what he is talking about. Nevertheless, for all the reasonable restraints and checks that lie upon us, there are eternal truths that need to be driven home—truths and judgments and values that are not here today and gone tomorrow, that will not have to be retracted when these years have passed. They do not "constitute an ethic connected with religion"; they are integral to it. They are "centered in Christ the Revealer" and derive from the experience and faith of the Christian community. They are more even than the bare will of God; they are compounded of that total process of redemption which is "antecedent to all ethics." They are themselves the many-splendored fact of Him Who in Christ reconciles the world unto Himself, *rescuing us from the power of the darkness and transferring us to*

The Realm of His Beloved Son*

That is the starting point of the Christian religion *as a way of life.*

What the church has to say, then, about the over-lordship of the state, whether the state be fascist or democratic; about human rights and the duties that go with them; about false and artificial economies of scarcity, with the fear and deceit and bitterness they breed; about all from-birth-to-grave techniques of security,—let her say it out of the fellowship and revelation, out of the Word and the salvation of God.

She will make for herself no easy friends [writes Bernard Iddings Bell] if she tells, as tell she must, those who would build the post-war world:

Your fine, new, mechanized, socialized, despiritualized culture is the work of children who have lost their way. It benefits nothing for mankind to master nature if the loss is the loss of human souls. Your gold is tarnished; your fine garments are moth-eaten; your rumbling cities are a pandemonium; you swarm like super-midges, you who were made to live like sons of God. You have forgotten the law of your being. The roots of peace lie deeper than your statesmen know. The one freedom that is indispensable, freedom from self, is not a thing to be achieved; it is the gift of One Whom man must permit to love him. We bring you tidings from Him.[7]

Even though men "stone the prophets and make the saints to suffer," let the church say this thing. Let her say it with no

* Colossians 1:13.

intent to sidestep her first responsibility to the separate souls of men. Let her say it with no intent to take refuge in action from that other and most irksome warning of Christ, *Verily, verily, I say unto thee, Except a man be born again, he cannot see the kingdom of God.* (John 3:3, A. V.) Let her say it with no slightest intent to beguile herself with any foolish hopes: as if, presto change, granted a new order, we should at once be able to grow new men in it; or as if by an equally miraculous transformation, granted men of good will, we should at once have a society of good will in which to operate. Let her say it not hastily or rashly, but bravely and humbly. Let her say it! By this, and not by oracular utterance in convention assembled; by the fearless and quiet discipline of an Incarnate Word, moving upon the living souls of men, shall God's Kingdom come. Call it the long road if you like. Some of those whose feet are most surely on it seem to think it is a hopeless and futile road. It may look so. God's roads sometimes do. But we are forever under the stern and adult necessity of traveling them if we mean to have anything at all of what we hope for,—a world more nearly like the world God meant. Perhaps then it shall be again, as it was in Charles Rand Kennedy's *The Terrible Meek*: When Force had long since done its worst on Calvary, a soldier watching looked at the day as it began to dawn around the cross and said, "It's coming light again." "Aye," answered the captain, "aye, it's coming light again—eternally!"

This surely is Paul's meaning when he writes to Timothy about

## Religion as a Force*

He saw the hard times that were coming when people would let it do no more than haunt the scenes of its ancient grandeur, worming its fatuous way into families—that is the shape it took then—and

* II Timothy 3:5.

getting hold of the womenfolk who felt crushed by the burden of their sins and were always curious to learn but never able to attain the knowledge of the truth (II Timothy 3:5, 6, 7). His is a picture for preachers to carry around with them. All that God can do is to help "poor creatures of impulse," whether they be optimistic liberals or pessimistic realists, to live through the nasty mess that makes the gift of His grace incongruous and renders the garnered energies of creation available only for the turning of private flutter-mills! That is why Christianity seems to be repudiated every time society drifts to the breaking point: because it wins for itself on one side or the other the name of impotence or the name of blind indifference, and it cannot afford either.

We have got to love the world enough to defy it again, exasperate it, make its smug complacencies miserable, sting its callous soul alive, rub to the quick if we must these flesh-and-blood situations and lay them quivering on the human conscience. What seems to me most subversive of all our hope at the present time is the almost irresistible tendency to fade completely into the general landscape for fear of running counter to something in it, so that our voice sounds precisely like the voice of the man in the street and the methods we proclaim are the methods he fashions. We have got to keep alive the tensions between that man's word and God's, instead of forever relaxing them. The Christian message, says Dr. Koechlin, President of the Swiss Church Federation, which for a long time seemed identical with the preaching of civic virtue and could not be heard as a directing, saving Word, is today becoming an absolute and is again received as a foolish or troublesome Word.[8] The whole secret of growth, the dynamic of historical change, lies in the continuing tautness of that encounter in the No Man's Land between what is and what God wills.

Here, for instance, is this matter of war. I beg of you not to flog it, pacifist or no pacifist. Out attitudes toward it, whatever they are, do not stand at the heart and center of the gospel. But do not sidestep it either. Personally I believe the time has come to assert the absolute of that other Will with regard to it: not just to say what everybody else is saying, not just to echo the changing voices of our generation. You may not agree. You may call such a point of view unrealistic if you like. It is realistic enough in this: it understands that the ultimate fact about human life is its solidarity. This jealous, divided occupancy of our disputed little earth is not God-appointed, and never was. What is God-appointed is the common needs, the common hopes, the common fears, of our common humanity. Sooner or later we have to come down to that. We are alive in a world where there is no longer any good that is our good, to be hedged about as if that were the way to defend it, or to be imposed on others as if that were the way to extend it. We are alive in a world where all we have is a trust, and where our use of it is what determines its survival, not the bulwarks and armies we throw around it. Turn, for instance, into a cheap license this freedom of which we are so jealous, and nothing will ever prevent the loss of it. But make it and keep it a clean glory among us, and nothing under God's sun will ever be strong enough to destroy it.

I am sure that it is not at all queer people like me with queer notions about war that constitute the danger spot in our democracy; it is the man who thinks that democracy is an unparalleled opportunity for him to get away with his own crooked practices in business and politics. He gets us so far into trouble that all the battleships and flying fortresses we can build will never blast a way out. We who call ourselves pacifists are not all liberals. We are not all utopians, unacquainted with the demonic force of evil. It is rather in reliance on the sover-eignty of God and on His chosen means that we take the stand we do; not with the hope of making friends of enemies, but in a kind of tortured obedience that will at least, unlike the easier processes of relativity, keep alive the strain between the will of God and this recurrent messiah of war, which leads us to ever "new disasters in the name of our own righteousness."

I would question insistently the oversimplification which identifies modern warfare with the legitimate use of force. I would question the claim that pacifism results inevitably in the cancellation of social responsibility. I would question the constantly repeated thesis that aid to weak and downtrodden humanity can be given in only one way. I would question the ethical validity of the statement that "exposing one's neighbor to the next blow" is the betrayal of all ethics. Christ exposed his followers, and plenty! God's own push in human history toward His goal of togetherness seems to be considerably "regardless of the direct good and evil involved."[9] Witness the present struggle!

It would seem to me far more likely that the rationalizing interventionist should turn out to be the liberal, the utopian, the idealist, alive in one world with his mind in another: alive in a world where spirit is decisive, with his mind in a world where force is his ultimate reliance. *While we look not at the things which are seen, but at the things which are not seen: for the things which are seen are temporal; but the things which are not seen are eternal* (II Corinthians 4:18, A.V.).

### III

May I point out at any rate that it is precisely in this creative character of the Christian religion, moving steadily away from man's will toward the will of God, that the romance lies, both of the Christian life and of Christian preaching? We have seen with what stirring, dynamic, adventurous truths we are to deal: the sovereignty and greatness of that Other; the incalculable dignity and worth of the human soul; the redemption from sin and death into life eternal, through our Lord Jesus Christ; the building of a truer, cleaner world in the Holy Name of the Most High. These are to be the matter of the modern pulpit. Surely, then, of themselves they should avail to lift the man in the pulpit out of drab, platitudinous mediocrity and dullness, into something that at least borders on the vivid and the elemental. However much he repeats—and repeat he must, if not himself, certainly this moving panorama of God in human life which is the gospel, varied but not various—let him constantly be aware that none of it needs to be commonplace or without color, "stale, flat, and unprofitable."

You will have noticed the zest which characterizes the whole swinging gait of the New Testament. *Never let your zeal flag*, writes Paul to the Romans. They were world-worn, too, I suppose.

### Maintain the Spiritual Glow

*Let your hope be a joy to you* (Romans 12:11, 12). It is the quality which life takes on, and preaching with it, when they both come surely under the swift, yare hands of God. Look at it in this tumbling, excited passage of Ephesians (3:20, 21) as it rushes pell-mell from the pen of a man who is some sixty years old: *Now to Him Who by the action of His power within us can do all things, aye, far more than we ever asked or imagined, to Him be glory in the church and in Christ Jesus throughout all generations forever and ever. Amen.* It is a Jew's exultant *Te Deum* after a life full of hardship, written from prison in the iron-fisted city of Rome, where they did not like Jews, and twenty centuries ago were none too careful, on the whole, about the manner of a Jew's demise!

I want you to stand it by the side of this other, for purposes of contrast. Here is a paragraph written a few years before the last war for one of our magazines by a young man of thirty-five, steadily, and in a measure interestingly, employed on the staff of a weekly business publication. He was sitting comfortably at his own desk, with the radio turned off,—his wife frequently enough, it would seem, in the same condition somewhere about the house. The stage was furnished quite pleasantly, and this is what comes of it:

I suspect there are a good many persons like me who are irritated more than soothed by the flow of life around them. I am up against a blank wall in a sense far more real than I care to admit. Evenings I get drunk, or rub the snout of my gregariousness against the fur of other animals about me, in an almost frantic effort to get relief from myself. Something has been taken out of me. The great majority of days are so filled with banality that all talk of purpose, meaning, and high morality seems a strange sort of cant.

*Now to Him Who can do all things, far more than we ever asked, to Him be glory throughout all generations forever and ever!* In whatever way you try to explain it, there is a difference between these two men which renders quite futile and abortive any attempt to gloss it over. They are living in widely separate worlds and they have little if anything in common. The aged and homeless apostle, with every reason to be churlish, is radiant; the young and home-weary editor, with every reason to be at least content, is surly and caustic. One of them was a Christian and meant his Christianity; his soul flamed with it. The other, this dweller in cities, our contemporary, without in the least understanding it, has decided that Christianity is quite too drab a business for him and has thrown it overboard so heartily that now he sits there biting his pencil and dully wondering what it is that has been taken out of him. The answer is not far to seek. He is minus religion and the creative zest that all true religion imparts to human life!

The unforgiveable sin of the pulpit, I submit, is to preach the kind of piety that stands around like a wallflower at a party, and nobody comes up and asks it to dance! It is clothed in a sacrificial air and wreathed in a dutiful smile. It tries to be very good and very helpful and succeeds only in being very negative and very much of a bore. It is stupid and uninteresting and has no appetite. It goes through the forms of godliness, but never does a blood-red thing for anybody. "It offers too little scope for freedom and adventure; there is not enough leeway for risks; not enough summons to courage. . . . By it men are made flabby; their skins are safe, but their morals are in danger."[10] Swinburne once described the impression it made on him: "Thou has conquered, O pale Galilean; the world has grown grey from thy breath." With its distressful duties, its laborious creeds, its tedious monotonies, it sets everybody who is really alive running as fast as ever he can in the opposite direction! I do not blame them. It has about the same effect on the average man that the late Alexander Woolcott once had.[11] They told him in his fraternity that his personal appearance was no great asset and that durin gthe rushing season he would do well to keep out of sight as much as possible. But he thought out for himself a road to sacrificial service, so he tells us. He deliberately perched himself on the empty porch of a rival fraternity house, his ungainly bulk clad in still more ungainly corduroys, and leaning over the rail with a sickly leer invited every passing freshman to come in and join. He almost succeeded in ruining the chapter!

It is sin that is dull and lifeless. For all the decoration some folk try to give it, it is a putrifying bit of gray carrion. Make that clear. Give its tedious business no advertisement by any complacent word or act of yours. It is unbelief that is tiresome, with the aimless litter it leaves behind it, finding nothing in this world but blind forces and mechanical results. I should as soon look for romance in a meat grinder. Religion is not drab. It is not an escape, a subtraction, a liability. It is not a therapy, making off hurriedly in the direction of poise and personality. It is a stirring, dynamic, adventurous thing. Preach it so. Let men see that it was intended to provide an outlet for the deepest urge of human life, which is just the desire to make things. Artists have that urge. Why else the frescoes on the walls of the monastery of San Marco in Florence? Authors have it. Why else *Macbeth* and *Hamlet* and *Othello* and *King Lear?* God had it. Why else are we here, and this vast place? We all have it. It is part of His image in us. In that of all things else are we most God-like. And Christianity was meant to serve it, so that of three sounds, as Browning put it, a man might be able to frame "not a fourth sound, but a star!"[12]

The fundamental joy of being a Christian consists not in being good. I get tired of that. But in standing with God against some darkness or some void and watching the light come. I remember how it was on a Sunday after church when a shy lad of eighteen opened for me one little window into the hell of loneliness that his soul was; and I saw after a while his face look out of it with laughter. The joy of religion is in having your fling, by the mercies of God, at shaping where you are, as a potter shapes a vase, one corner of His eternal Kingdom. It is in chiseling out of the crude granite of the world "carved angels, eager-eyed, with hair blown back, and wings put crosswise on their breasts, choir over choir, with face to face uplifted."

And on it the apostle rests his case. *I appeal to you, too,*
As a Worker with God

*do not receive the grace of God in vain* (II Corinthians 6:1). All this sum total of God's varied attributes: the depth of His wisdom and the length of His patience; the clarity of His justice and the fullness of His mercy; the gallantry of that ruthless love which spared

neither itself nor its objects; and the steadiness of the Power
that sits unshaken on the Throne of the World, ruling the
skies off with a span, measuring the waters in the hollow of His
hand, and with His jewelers' scales the mountains as if they
were dust (Isaiah 40:12). All that for nothing; and the Voice
that keeps saying, *Think not of the far past, dwell not on the
deeds of old; here is a new deed of mine springing to light—
have you no eyes for it?"* (Isaiah 43:18, 19) All that come to
nothing! Paul could not imagine it. He was not afraid God
would waste anything. He was afraid that people would waste
God and life would grow intolerable.

It will when this war is over if we do not look sharp. You
will have to face a worn-out world, by the side of which my
world was brilliant; its flame burned down, its passion doubly
disillusioned. However will you manage? Listen once more to
this young editor as he sat there disconsolately in the midst of
a landscape that seemed somehow so strangely faded. Toward
the end of his article he tells us what it is he is dreaming:

It seems to me that the essential source of my trouble is a need for
some unshakable conviction of the importance of living, and of the
way a man should live. In strong measure I am fascinated by the
incalculable. There should be some adventure and uncertainty in
life. I prefer to pit myself against hazardous moments, to try myself
to the utmost, to have the greatest possible variety out of my
journey from the hamlet of birth to the City of Death.

And one listens breathlessly, hardly understanding how anybody could come so near the habit and temper of Jesus and the
very core of his gospel and still be unconscious of it. If Christianity was not tailor-made to fit that, what is, or ever has been?

The sermon that will win for itself a hearing when all our
zest for killing has died down is the sermon that can bring with
it, straight from this Galilean, some "unshakable conviction of
the importance of living"; confront our worn-out world with

the incalculable, with One Who is less a rock than a spirit, like the wind in your sail, whipping up the salt spray from the crest of the waves and flinging it in your face. It is Christ who has things to say about man and God and human destiny that cannot be wrong, they are too eternally right; who cared enough to hold out his hand to a blind beggar; who was willing to do anything to keep men from turning up their nose at the life which he thought was so unspeakably great, and which so many others, by thinking as he thought, have made unspeakably beautiful.

Back in January, 1943, an old negro died. Every morning at four o'clock he would kneel down by his bed and ask for his marching orders from God. He wanted to know what man was; but God said that was too big. So he began asking about life; but that, too, God told him, was too big. Finally, he came down with his questions. "Tell me then," said he, "about the peanut and the sweet potato." And God said that while He could not tell him all about them, they were indeed more his size. Now his mother had been a slave, and his father, too. Nearly eighty years ago she had looked down on his tiny black face in a miserable hut. His name was George. One day he himself added Washington, to make it read George Washington Carver. And the marching orders began coming in!

Stand men on their feet in front of that God Whose mysterious world will never let them count on anything except that they are going to be surprised at the way He will work it out if they let Him. Until all you have to say becomes itself an adventure in living under the spell of Him who still sends out His own, two by two, with no scrip, no bread, no money, nothing for their journey but a staff and some shoes; still tells them to expect persecution; still smiles proudly at them because they not only are, but are willing to be, lambs among wolves. Is that tame? And under the spell of this strange land beneath the stars, with all there is in it that has to be set right, and the risks you can run!

Not Herod, [writes Dorothy Sayers] not Caiaphas, not Pilate, not Judas ever contrived to fasten upon Jesus Christ the reproach of insipidity; that final indignity was left for pious hands to inflict. To make of his story something that could neither startle, nor shock, nor terrify, nor excite, nor inspire a living soul is to crucify the Son of God afresh and put him to an open shame. . . . Let me tell you, good Christian people, an honest writer would be ashamed to treat a nursery tale as you have treated the greatest drama in history.[13]

*It is no weak Christ* you worship. It is *a Christ of power* (II Corinthians 13:3).

Let no sermon, therefore, be without the sound of a trumpet. The devil was asked once what he missed most about heaven, and that was it: the sound of God's trumpets in the morning. And people miss it, too. They know. They are not brave enough; that is all. "They talk down what they dare not be." They know very well, from their own few and hesitating and cautious experiments with it, what amazing and impossible strength this gospel calls for, what steadfastness it demands, how it comes out again and again on a lonely hill, hardly to be distinguished from the fate that overtakes some of the wicked. So they try to be rid of it by treating it on occasion as if it were a fairy story, and arguing very intellectually that it is! Like the inhabitants of Chartres, who wanted once to destroy their glorious cathedral, because it "dominated offensively their foolish little city." "I prefer to pit myself against hazardous moments!" Very well. If anybody happens to mean it, let him look around. There are enough people yet who will cheat him for being honest, and hurt his feelings if he shows himself affectionate! But nobody wants you to stop playing that reveille. It is not Christianity that is tiresome; it is what we make it. It is not Jesus of Nazareth who bores men; it is their everlasting effort to dodge him down the road of their own convenience.

Speaking of this grace of God, you remember how Paul wrote in his second letter to the Corinthians of what he called his thorn in the flesh, something he wanted terribly to get rid of, some ailment, some weakness, something; so that he prayed about it once, again, and yet again. Only, nothing happened, except that God kept saying to him, *It is enough for you to have My grace* (II Corinthians 12:9). That word "enough" has always amused me a little. It sounds so much as if God were trying to be very modest about it all, promising a grace just level with a man's need. And here it is, some ten years later, in the letter to Timothy: *The grace of our Lord flooded my life* (I Timothy 1:14). It was not "enough." It was not up to the brim at all. It was a broken dam.

*Not the grace of God—in vain!* Anything else, not that! Turning dinosaurs into lizards that a man can kick around with his foot! Satisfied to set this incomparably great thing such meager tasks, content to reap from it the meager harvests we reap! Employing the "universe to rear a lily-of-the-valley!"[14]

## IV

And yet more vital by far than even this creative zest of the Christian life is the age-long background of Christian worship out of which it springs. Nothing is more conspicuous in the New Testament. Take only Paul's epistle to the Romans. Somebody, I think it was Dr. Jowett, said he was like a lark, building his nest close to the ground, but darting away to Heaven with his song. To me this letter of his is more like one of Bach's fugues or the Hallelujah Chorus, rolling back again and again from all its lesser forms and movements to its swelling theme: *Blessed forevermore be the God who is over all* (Romans 9:5). Then ending with it, whether by his hand or another's, in a great burst of music,

To the Only Wise God Be Glory*

This it is, if I
may change the figure for a moment, that keeps the flame of
his life burning, supplies it with air, keeps it clear blue. *A name
above all names, so that before the name of Jesus every knee
should bend in heaven, on earth, and underneath the earth, and
every tongue confess that "Jesus Christ is Lord," to the glory of
God the Father. Therefore, my beloved, . . . work all the more
strenuously, . . . for it is God who . . . enables you to will
this and to achieve it* (Philippians 2:9–13).

To speak, then, of the relationship between Christian service
and Christian worship hardly even makes sense. There is no
possibility of division between them, any more than there is of
division between doing and being. They are one true perpetual
act. Of that act the sermon at its best is a kind of vehicle. If it
fails as the instrument of either, it fails. It is to bring people to
their knees, but not to leave them there. Their wings shall
stretch forth; but toward the mercy-seat shall their faces be
(Exodus 25:20 A.V.).

Here, roughly, it seems to me, is the principal difference
between a teacher and a preacher, between a lecture and a
sermon. The one explains, the other at best must fashion. The
one instructs, the other at best induces. The one points, the
other at best provides. The teacher informs; the lecturer may
exhort. The preacher does more. In the words of Georeg Stewart, his is "a celebration of the goodness and dignity and love of
God." What he says does not go hand in hand with worship or
break in on it for a while. What he says occasions worship and
provokes it. He does not discuss peace; he gives it birth. He
does not point the way to strength; he ministers strength.

None of it is accomplished by means of decorative and
rhetorical devices. None of it is accomplished by striving, as if
you were to say, "Go to, this day I shall preach and lead the

* Romans 16:27.

gaunt souls of men into the satisfying presence of the Most
High." The sermon must reveal God. Watch Second Isaiah
coming back to that desperately, over and over. Without it he
can do nothing, stir nobody. Show God to your people, and
they will worship. The only thing they need is to be shown.
Show them nothing else, not yourself, not some error, not some
truth, not the deep pathos of their lives, but God.

There is a story of Leonardo da Vinci, and of how in the
first painting of the "Last Supper" he had put such pains and
such a wealth of detail into two cups standing on the table
that a friend, seeing them, stared at them in open-mouthed
amazement; whereupon the artist seized a brush and with one
sweep of his hand painted them out of the picture, crying as he
did it, "Not that! That isn't what I want you to see! It's the
Face. Look at the Face!"[15]

Show men God, and they will come; they will come as if
under some profound constraint to do Him their obeisance.
Even the stranger may not scoff. Recall that scene in I Corinthians: *Rather shall the secrets of his heart be brought to
light; and he shall fall on his face and worship, his wondering
eyes bearing witness, and his sobered lips confirming it, de-
claring*

God Is Really among You*

Surely then the sermon above all else will be reverent. I have
never thought a sparing use of humor inappropriate. A man, it
seems to me, may worship God at times even with a light and
merry heart. But unless somehow your humor contributes to
the end purpose of bringing up the human soul in solemn salu-
tation of the Divine, it is not only inappropriate; it is an abomination of desolation standing in the holy place. So is every profane attempt at the kind of oratory which is the substitution of
words for ideas, when a man just shines his eyes and opens his
mouth and leaves the rest to God! Together with all ranting

* I Corinthians 14:23-25.

and poundings on the pulpit! The Lord gave me my authority, writes Paul, *for building you up, not for demolishing you* (II Corinthians 10:8; 13:10). I will not be lashed into any love if you please, nor will anyone else, crack your whip ever so loudly! Not in the wind, not in the earthquake, not in the fire, but in a Voice; and the burden of that Voice is *Be still,* quit your noise, throw down your wilful arms,—that is what it means— *and know that I am God!* (Psalm 46:10 A.V.)

Nor may anyone lose sight of the setting given the sermon in the surrounding service.

Let Everything Be Done Decorously and in Order*

These matters are not preliminary or introductory; they are of the essence. The whole atmosphere in which the sermon must live and move and have its being is from first to last a matter of the gravest concern.

There is the music. I find that organists often forget their function, lose sight of the fact that music is not an end in itself but a medium of worship, and take advantage of every opportunity to play a few connecting phrases, or to show off the organ and their own skill, with the quality of the voices they have singing with them. The result is decoration, something that is obtrusive, calls attention to itself, parades in front of you from the choir stalls with its thumbs in its armholes. Arias and oratorios would far better be left to the stage for which they were written, their place taken by the simpler, devotional forms that bring up a soul with bowed head before the glory of God.

The hymns should make their own contribution to the unity of the whole and move with a certain dignity. I should not always be making concessions, if I were you, to popular taste. That taste was tested recently in a sort of poll. It runs all the way from "Jesus, Lover of My Soul," "Rock of Ages," "The Church's One Foundation," to the Moody and Sankey variety,

* I Corinthians 14:40.

such as "The Ninety and Nine" and "The Battle Hymn of the Republic," with its rollicking refrain, "Glory, Glory, Hallelujah." It was about this second group that Dr. Williamson of the Westminster School was speaking when he said that all those hymns to which we are irresistibly drawn to beat time, all of them that get, so to speak, into our feet, are essentially secular; and of them during the last century there has been a nauseating abundance. To allow congregations to be fast wedded to them is not a concession to the needs of the average person, but a surrender to what is often enough "sheer vulgarity," coprophagy. An occasional study of the noblest, most august hymns of the church, and of the distinguished collections of them that have been made quite recently by a number of denominations in their new and revised hymnals, would prove one of the most rewarding of courses in any program of adult education.

So, too, in the matter of fixed orders for worship. A great deal of progress has lately been made backwards, it seems to me, to the ancient liturgies of the church. The extemporaneous in our common American practice has taught us much by way of reality, and I know its value; but I know its dangers as well. All things may be lawful, as the apostle has said, but not all are good for us! (I Corinthians 10:23) Certainly not that oppressive sense of immediacy which always hovers over the spur of the moment. I for one believe that in just measure we need the continuity of great tradition, and that ineffable perfume of the long and steady devotion of past ages, which is the prayers of the saints: not that God is "preoccupied with His dignity" and "obscure as to what He wants His subjects to do;" but simply lest the whole service seem to be taken indoors off the street, with none of that quality about it which would proclaim it to be in the world and yet somehow not of the world.

Certainly, none of it, if it goes on in a setting of general confusion, can be of any value. I have heard ministers battling about hopelessly at the altar trying to achieve a victory lost already in the aisles and among the pews. Noisy and indecorous ushers, chatty friends, pompous, obtrusive deacons, organists, sextons, thoughtless youngsters from the Bible school,—there are times and places and people that seem to defy the spirit of worship, and put it dismally to rout. With quietness and courtesy, with gentleness and persistence, we need to transform them. To teach reverence and to practice it is a far more important part of our task as ministers of the Gospel than some of us seem to think.

We must practice it in our speech and bearing all the days, and practice it in the chancel by our conduct of the service. One of the most vivid images left in my memory of those rare occasions when it has been my privilege to worship with others in the pew is the image of a certain minister paging assiduously through his prayer-book while his assistant led in the Confession of Sin, and a moment later peering about over the congregation during the reading of the lessons. I can think of nothing more inexcusable. One can forgive a man for not being a great preacher; but one has no call to forgive a man for careless sacrilege, and that is what such indignities are. There are communions already blessed with a wealth of liturgy,—and it is wealth, until people begin to use it as an end in itself; then it is chaff and refuse. To rattle through it lifelessly, with no understanding of its scope and immensities; or on the other hand to clothe it with a pious and pulpit manner, trying with false solemnity in ministerial, pontifical tones to "talk like God"—this is to set up a barrier sometimes wholly insurmountable between earth and heaven, between the dryness of many days and the refreshment of still waters.

Let Scripture always be read with care and intelligence, and never without a previous studied reading, lest men see for themselves that the words are going in at our eyes and coming out at our mouth without ever passing through our mind. *Under-*

*standest thou what thou readest?* asked Philip of the eunuch (Acts 8:30 A. V.). Then give your lips to it. Read it so that others may understand it. Read it naturally, and earnestly, not as if you had written it for your own proprietary distribution, but like a man who is listening;[16] not as one who knows the psalm but as one who knows the shepherd![17] To pray, instead of repeating prayers. In all things to move simply and speak directly, bowing your own head in spirit and in truth, yourself building an "honest altar" and invoking "the sacred fire."[18]

This it is to join hands with all nations, and kindreds, and people, and tongues, before the Throne and before the Lamb, clothed with white robes and with palms in their hands, saying, "Blessing and glory and wisdom and thanksgiving and honor and power and might be unto our God forever and ever"; and with angels and archangels to laud and magnify His glorious name. This it is to set one great hour against the background of eternity and worship there with others, until the knowledge of God's glory in the face of Jesus Christ (II Corinthians 4:6) doth that day invade and lay hold on human lives. Let it be so; that we, in whose sober charge God has placed His honor, may out of the dust of common ways set a rainbow in the heavens and the pattern of a Father's face against the sky.

> For worship
>       is a thirsty land crying out for rain,
> It is a candle in the act of being kindled,
> It is a drop in quest of the ocean,
>
> .      .      .      .      .      .
>
> It is a voice in the night calling for help,
> It is a soul standing in awe before the mystery of the
>       universe,
>
> .      .      .      .      .      .
>
> It is time flowing into eternity,
>    . . . a man climbing the altar stairs to God.[19]

And God moving down!

Industry in Art is a necessity, not a virtue, and any evidence of the same . . . a blemish, not a quality. . . . Work alone will efface the footsteps of work.

JAMES McNEILL WHISTLER

✓✓✓✓✓✓✓✓✓✓✓✓✓✓✓✓✓✓✓✓✓✓✓✓✓✓✓✓✓✓✓✓✓✓✓✓✓✓✓✓✓✓✓✓✓

# Chapter 5

## A SOUND WORKMAN

✓✓✓✓✓✓✓✓✓✓✓✓✓✓✓✓✓✓✓✓✓✓✓✓✓✓✓✓✓✓✓✓✓✓✓✓✓✓✓✓✓✓✓✓✓

In this chapter and the next we arrive at our destination. Such at least is my hope! With a hurried survey of the world around us, as one would glance about a room, we turned at once to the preacher's task, and then to the man inside it. After that we attempted to get out in the clear as nearly as we could with regard to the content of preaching. Next we asked with what authority we could come, touching on the creative function of the Christian religion and observing its background in Christian worship. Now we gird our loins to do the thing about which we have been talking and straightway get down to the final business of preparing and delivering a sermon.

May I give voice here at the very beginning to what another has said but I would repeat with profound conviction: that the first step toward a good sermon is hard word, the second step is more hard work, and the third is still more. *Do your utmost,* writes Paul to Timothy, *to let God see that you at least are a sound workman,*

With No Need to Be Ashamed*

Heaven help the man of us who discovers that he is a ready speaker and presumes to rely on it! The years will undo him and let him down. His undisciplined mind will little by little fall back on "sound and fury," signifying nothing. The sermons he keeps shaking out of his sleeve will soon begin to bring the lining with them, as a dear friend of mine once phrased it (and he was himself no little given to such legerdemain!) It makes no difference how readily preaching comes to you, how quick your wit, how facile your flow of language; you may be "the spiritual speakeasy of America." I beg you never allow yourself to be betrayed into indolence by any such thing. For him who does, the day of reckoning is already on the march; his doom will answer to his deeds (II Corinthians 11:15), and cry his poverty aloud for all who will to hear and cover their faces at his shame. You need never spend any time envying the man who can stand up on his two feet and do extemporaneously what you can hardly do after days of laborious writing. Often enough to suit your weary soul he will turn out to be the rabbit the tortoise overtook. His very faculties will become his difficulties. I have learned to know, from some little acquaintance with preachers who have something to say, what unremitting toil preaching costs the men who not only illustrate the ministry but adorn it; and I myself am singularly comforted. If I have to carry around with me for the rest of my life a plodding mind that wants anywhere from eighteen or twenty hours to thirty before it is willing to have me get up in the pulpit, at least I do

* II Timothy 2:15.

not have to be afraid that what I am pleased to call my intellectual machinery will grow rusty and break down from disuse, or that some day I shall have to pay across the counter in still more vapid mouthings and platitudinous banalities the price of all laziness, however able it may be.

Precisely in this connection I have often wondered just how much the modern distaste for sermons and the not uncommon disregard, to put it no more strongly, which people have for preachers—especially the people who keep continually announcing themselves as the arbiters of thought and conduct—I have often wondered just how much of all this is due to our own lethargy and dull sloth. We like to blame it on the spirit of the age, or on the everlasting perversity of human nature, when frequently the plain fact is, much as we dislike to admit it, that we have not put into our sermons the muscle and the sweat it takes to hold human eyes and human ears to anything anywhere. It takes muscle and sweat to paint, whether you are painting a picture or painting a fence. It takes muscle and sweat if you are bent on singing a song or writing an editorial or pulling a guinea pig out of a silk hat. It takes muscle and sweat to write a sermon. To fasten a man's attention and challenge his respect is not done lightly, no matter how worthy your material or how exalted your theme.

Years ago an elderly minister gave one of my assistants his advice. It was brought to me with glee. "Your sermons," he said, "don't have to be interesting." That would be a great solace to many if it were only true. But John the Baptist was never dull. I should be willing to stake a good deal on that. Nor was Jesus. Nor was Paul, except perhaps that one time when he got tangled up in poetry and philosophy on Mars' Hill—?—to his own later profit.[1] "Begin with Scripture," went on this minister's counsel, "and end with Scripture. Fill up the middle of it with Scripture." As for me, "I fear the man of one book; he is usually a bore."[2] Some of us are altogether too much inclined to claim for this truth which is God's the hearing it deserves; and always it gets only the hearing we can win for it. Throwing together a few impeccable heads of discourse, thrashing about among them with some sober doctrine as with a flail, then trying to bind the fragments with a few passages of Holy Writ,—this is never enough to justify either the man or his message. Nothing is enough except it be "all that is within you," which indeed is what you have promised.

Even then the crowds may pass you by. For to be honest and diligent and above reproach in your study is not necessarily to be a popular preacher. In fact, often enough to be worthy at least of some passing note, it is quite the contrary. Dr. Harris Kirk, of Baltimore, to whose great capacity for friendship I have long been a debtor, gave me much balm from Gilead by insisting that truly great preaching never is and never has been popular. It seemed somehow to take the sting out of the crowds some others drew. And to explain those "little handfuls scattered in a spacious building, betaking themselves in furtive fashion to the farthest corners,"[3] which in those days so often turned out to be my own congregation. But, of course, within limits he was right; though it must be remembered that the unpopularity of the truth is one thing, and the unpopularity of a dawdler and a sluggard is another thing entirely. We may not be very good as preachers; but we owe it to God, we owe it to the truth, we owe it to our people, and we owe it to ourselves, to be as good as we are. That way, and no other, some day we shall be better. *Shun any brother who is loafing* (II Thessalonians 3:6).

### Stick to Your Work*

Now this preparation for preaching is of two kinds. There is the kind that begins away back in the past somewhere and continues steadily through the years. It is the kind which was in James Black's thought when he wrote with such earnestness, albeit with some confu-

\* I Timothy 4:16.

sion of metaphor, that good preaching is "the natural overflow of a ripe mind." Then there is that kind of preparation which begins when the threat or promise of next Sunday falls like a shadow or a song across the week. Generalities can go hang then. Something specific has to happen.

Variety number one, which begins back in the past somewhere, would certainly do well, while about it, to begin with one's grandparents, or even better. The men who come into the ministry from homes where true piety and genuine culture have long been a family tradition fall heir to an advantage which is quite incalculable; and this for their sobering, to an accountability before God and at the bar of human life which matches that advantage in breadth, depth, and height.

But not all of us can start so long ago. We have no such heritage. There was little ancestral culture perhaps. Only an average piety. Traditions of the farm, it may be, the shop, the craft, the store. These, shall we say, constitute our background. We hardly fit into it any more. We stand out against it in a kind of relief, part of it, but different; like it somehow, yet strangely other. We are the first of our blood in professional life. My sole insistence, then, is that what we lack behind the scenes we do deliberately make up, or attempt to, when once we are ushered on the stage to shift for ourselves. We are to fashion our own advantages. We are to create and cultivate our own tastes. We are to set our own lofty standards. We are to be the pioneers of our strain; not content with minimum requirements, with narrow outlooks, with inherited prejudices. Every effort must be made to broaden the horizons of life; to push out the boundaries of normal human experience; to extend our knowledge of literature, of language, of science, and of the arts: *to make the man of God proficient* (II Timothy 3:17). In short, we have to amass in one generation the wealth of three! And it can be done. It has been done. A crude, inept, and uninformed preacher, with but few acquaintances among the great minds of the past and but a poor appetite for the best things of the present, is not just a sad victim of heredity or the pathetic product of an unfortunate environment; he has had something to do with it himself.

The nature of that steady regimen to which all of us, some perhaps more than others, must of necessity submit ourselves, I can only indicate. Let me say first of all that we are not to be omnivorous devourers of newspaper print. I am deeply persuaded that the time we spend with it in excess of fifteen or twenty minutes is wasted time. John Hutton used to advise that we stand up while reading it and lay it aside when we are tired. Some such counsel is "worthy of all acceptation." Once that is over and letters are answered, you may sit down immediately and, while yet fresh, launch into the appointed schedule of reading and study. *That your love,* writes Paul, *may be*
More and More Rich in Knowledge
*and all manner of insight* (Philippians 1:9). He understood that there is a way to God down the corridors of the mind. Give yourself to that as a man would give himself into custody. Let your congregation know, tactfully, at the outset of your ministry, that your habitual and unfailing practice is to devote yourself to study for some stated period each day; and you will find, I think, that they will not only understand but will give you their hand on it. Nothing is truer than that an idle minister is soon discovered and never wanted. Men visit him with a "swift contempt." There are few if any who ever fail to win the sympathetic support of their people in the determination rigorously to keep for their own sober use those first precious hours of the morning. It has been suggested somewhere that we need only tell them the story of "The Man from Porlock" who dropped in one day to see Coleridge, on what trifling business no one knows, and drove from his mind the whole vision of Kubla Khan!

With regard to the character and content of one's reading it seems to me that some of it not alone may be but ought to be purely and simply for enjoyment. Books as frivolous as detective stories. I have always cherished dark misgivings about the brethren who do not like them! Other books, light, and yet no doubt a shade more profitable: as, for instance, the best of the novels, classical and modern; collections of essays, biographies, poetry. As far as I am concerned, this type of reading can best be done in the evening, or at the fag end of things. Sometimes I lull myself to sleep with it at night.

Next in importance is the discriminating use of periodicals, secular and religious. One rarely needs to spend more than an hour on any of them. They are often my subway reading. Then that more serious and sober program in history and the sciences, in philosophy and theology, with the excitement of which Christopher Morley writes in "The Haunted Bookshop." "Those shelves," says the proprietor, pointing to the walls, "are ranked with the most furious combustibles in the world, the brains of men. . . . Surround a man with Carlyle, Emerson, Thoreau, Chesterton, Shaw, Nietzsche; would you wonder at his getting excited? What would happen to a cat if she had to live in a room tapestried with catnip? She would go crazy!"

It is no dull or dutiful task. And more rewarding than any of it is the continued and systematic study of the Bible, book by book. I am never accused anywhere else with so insistent a finger. Nowhere else does God seem so great or life so meaningful, with compelling hands to lay hold on you. I have spent summers, whole years, in a review of the Gospels and the epistles; in these latter days particularly the prophets: more frequently by way of specific sermon-preparation, but not solely to that end.

All such reading, I would suggest, with of course the creative work of writing, should be held over for those cleanest, clearest hours when the mind is most vigorous and the will least fatigued. With no more complicated an arrangement than this, it is amazing what can be accomplished, provided only there be some decent measure of steadiness and industry. It is terrifying to find how utterly disrupting both morally and intellectually is a haphazard, straggling, dislocated day; whereas, to set aside even an hour out of twenty-four and regularly devote it to reading is to add to the list of your "familiars" something more than a book a week.

In no case is there much excuse for the facts recorded recently in *The New York Times* as the result of a survey made by the librarian of Cooper Union. It was reported with some satisfaction:

The reading habits of clergymen are slovenly, without plan or discipline, and fall short of the standard one would expect of a group with such high educational background and so rich an opportunity for intellectual leadership.

Nearly all the one hundred twenty-two ministers answering the questionnaire complained of the lack of opportunity and the burden of parish duties. Much has since been said in their defense by sympathetic editors. But little is to be had from offering excuses to life. Life never stamps them "valid." Mastery of our time may not always be possible. When everything is said and done, you and I are men under authority and cannot command our days; yet to lose a battle need not be to lose a whole campaign. One morning ruthlessly torn out of your hands and away from its original purpose by some necessity that does not ask your leave may still be made up, hour for hour, if you really mean this ledger of yours to balance.

And do, for your own mind's sake, with an eye, too, to the minds of those who are expected to listen when you speak, do keep one book going that is just a bit beyond you. There is very meager profit to be had from reading what you yourself might well have written. It is good for a man to get his teeth into something that is tough. Polite society may shudder, as one advertisement used to have it, but the dentist will applaud. Stand within reach of your chair von Hügel's *Essays and Addresses,* Otto's *Idea of the Holy,* Kierkegaard, possibly Temple's *Nature, Man and God,* or Dixon's *The Human Situation,* surely Berdyaev's *Freedom and the Spirit,* Farmer's *The World and God, The Servant of the Word,* Weber's *The Protestant Ethic,* and surely, too, Skinner's *Prophesy and Religion,* Niebuhr's *The Nature and Destiny of Man,* and Kenneth Kirk's *The Vision of God.* Name others as you will. Theological book reviews and supplements appear every year by the score, to add to the list; while publications in Great Britain are announced from time to time through the columns of *The Christian News-Letter.* Make your choice and have one or two always on hand. Perhaps you can develop the adult educational projects of your church to such an extent that your own part in them will compel your faithfulness to certain scholarly pursuits and interests. By whatever device, may you be held fast by an unforgiving discipline! For when those interests flag and faint, the gate yawns wide into the valley of dry bones and the bell begins to toll. Ask not for whom!

And never as you read, night or morning, be without paper and pen. A pen, because penciled notes soon blur and become so unattractive and illegible as to be practically worthless. The clear and quick recording of illustrations; the copying out of quotations; the jotting down of some fleeting, suggestive line of thought: such material carefully gathered, preserved, perhaps even entered in a permanent book, not too laboriously indexed, is simply invaluable. It took me altogether too long to learn that: I have lost a hundred sermons. I still lose them. I wish I could persuade you to begin with it and save time. You will have to find your own system. But stick to it. Stick to it when it irks you. Stick to it when the going gets thick. Stick to it when the stuff grows thin. Stick to it. The effort itself, if nothing else comes of it, will prove an aid to memory. And maybe some day you will not be a slave to *The Preacher's Manual* for your themes and anecdotes, or to the last issue of *The Christian Century Pulpit!*

My only point here is that from such preliminary and constant groundwork alone does the harvest grow, and from the contacts we make the while with human hopes and human fears. It is out of such deliberate and constant application that sermons are born, themes suggest themselves, illustrations leap up, points march out waving banners, new and larger understandings dawn. John Hutton tells of how his mind, as it runs along the ways of that discipline, flings little bits of truth at him, of insight, of spiritual observation, in a kind of ill-natured manner, as if it were saying, "You're always at me for this sort of thing; very well, there you are." And forthwith he takes out his pen and paper and thanks his grumpy master by setting down and honoring and making much of these, its sudden offers of power.[4] So does one come upon the source of his freshness, of that quality of his preaching which usually goes by the name of originality. It is ever so. "Ideas," writes old Samuel Butler in *The Way of All Flesh,* and it is a lesson worth learning,—"ideas no less than the living beings in whose minds they arise, must be begotten by parents not very unlike themselves. They do not come into clever people's heads by a kind of spontaneous generation, without parentage in the thoughts of others or the course of observation. The very worst method of getting hold of them is to go hunting expressly after them."

To say it bluntly for ourselves, ideas are like happiness: they come along some road, rarely at the end of any. They spring from broad acres and big, well-cultivated farms, for the folk who are more than weekly opportunists, Monday's "moody gleaners, searching for thin ears."[5] All of us, I dare say, have at one time or another looked forward with something like terror to the long succession of Sundays stalking toward us out of the future, each with its own demand for two or more sermons. Where on earth could anybody find themes enough? To take up the whole task and stare at it from that end makes it seem unendurably huge. But there are, too, always six days before Sunday comes. For my part, where I have been faithful and diligent, there in my commonplace book, or deep somewhere in my heart are things waiting to be said, holding out their hands to me pleadingly. And I choose from among them. Some of them have been gathering notes and comments around themselves for months, as a stone gathers accretions through the years; others are mere suggestions, similarities, contrasts, what the physicist would perhaps call fields of force.

It may be, for instance, that a friend calls your attention, as one did mine,[6] to those three towering questions in the third chapter of Genesis: *Hath God indeed said . . . ?* Here is an evil spirit persuading somebody to tamper with the eternal order of things as if it were neither an order nor eternal, until the man stands there ashamed among the trees, quite lost. *Adam, Adam, where art thou?* He is altogether at his wits' end, because he has run away after some poorer counsel than God's. Then softer comes again this voice from heaven. *Who told thee that thou wast naked?* And we here listening must say to one another, "Who, indeed, if not that ineffable Word of God itself made flesh?"

Or you glance down at the fourth chapter of the same book: And the Lord said unto Cain, *"Where is Abel, thy brother?"* Berdyaev says that morality began with that question, but reaches its fulfillment in this: when God puts it to the good man about the bad; to the man who is up and in, about the man who is down and out; to the religious man about the pagan; to the righteous man about the wicked; saying, "Abel, Abel, where is thy brother Cain?"

Or shall we say on another morning you read of Moses, how he *wist not that his face shone* (Exodus 34:29, A.V.). And then of Samson (Judges 16:20, A.V.), how he *wist not that the Lord was departed from him.* Two men, God almost visible in one and quite gone from the other, and neither conscious of what has happened. As in that twenty-fifth chapter of Matthew: *Then shall the King say to those on his right . . . , "I was hungry and you fed me"; . . . and the just will answer, "Lord, when?" Then he will say to those on the left, "I was hungry but you never fed me . . ."* and *they will answer him too, "Lord, when?"* (vss. 35, 37; 42, 44) Destiny forever shaping itself toward laughter or toward tears, and that day coming which Amos said was *darkness, and not light* (5:18, A.V.), coming like a thief, stealing furtively across the grass, no more than another shadow where the shadows are deepest. *Moses wist not. Samson wist not.* Nobody conscious of the things that matter most! *Lord, when?*

Perhaps in this same Book of Judges another text catches your eye and begins stalking through the corridors of your mind. In the King James Version it reads, *But the spirit of the Lord came upon Gideon* (Judges 6:34). In the Hebrew, *the spirit of the Lord clothed himself with Gideon.* You jot it down, for you mean to preach on it sometime: poor human flesh, and the might of the Lord wearing it like a vestment, throwing it about Him, as one would fling a cloak, and striding toward His own great ends. I preached on it once, and it didn't work!

Some other day, over in the New Testament in Luke, you come upon that child who is *set for the fall and rising again of many in Israel* (2:34, A.V.). All the weakness is on one side; an infant that could not even keep the fluttering breath of life in its own body. And all the might of the world is on the other. But the odds are with this little fragment of humanity. Your theme becomes God's Weakness and Man's Might. Or again, in the eleventh chapter is that story of Christ's quick response to the woman whose eyes must have brimmed over with tears as she clasped her hands to her breast and cried out for everybody to hear, *Blessed is the womb that bare Thee* (verse 27, A.V.). It was like saying, "How happy your mother must be and how proud to have a son like you!" And Jesus leaped back as if a chasm had opened at his feet. *Yea rather,* he answered, *happy are they that hear the Word of God, and keep it.* Later it may be you will preach on Hard Answers to Soft Sayings.

Perhaps you are on Calvary. Pray God you are often there. And you hear that cry, *My God, My God, why hast Thou forsaken me?* (Matthew 27:46) The whole text in Matthew reminds you of the twenty-second psalm. It seems to you that Jesus must have meant it all; he knew it by heart.[7] Read it and see. You may catch the note of triumph better and know more surely what God meant in Isaiah (65:24) : *Before they call, I will answer; and while they are yet speaking, I will hear.* Where else was it ever truer than on that little hill outside the city wall?

Let us suppose that one evening you have been reading Eugene O'Neill's weird drama, *Lazarus Laughed.* The theme of it is man's fear of life, not death, and it keeps haunting you. It begins to associate itself with a word from the gospel: *And they went out quickly, and fled from the sepulchre; for they trembled and were amazed: neither said they anything to any man; for they were afraid* (Mark 16:8, A.V.). You begin to wonder if that empty tomb has suddenly made their world too small. Is that why men are afraid to live? Has their world been upset because eternity has been put at its heart, to turn all its bargains, its careful bargains, shoddy? Or has this empty tomb suddenly made them too great, so that they are dizzy at being sudden giants, having to live bravely now instead of stooping about so ridiculously, not as little as they wished to be, but as big as they are? So the thought grows and fits itself into the Easter story.

Still again, you are browsing around through your *Expositor's Greek Testament* and come on James 1:22: *Be ye doers of the word, and not hearers only,*—so goes the Authorized Version. Then all at once, as if you had never seen it before, that Greek word for "doers," *poietai,* calls up another word, "poet," as The

Witch of Endor calls up Samuel's ghost! And you begin planning a sermon on The Christian Life as Poetry, with the familiar painting of Alma Tadema before the eyes of your memory, a lad lying prone on the ground in a garden, dreaming of great deeds as he listens to a reading from Homer. *Not hearers, doers,* —yourselves, poets!

So do themes come knocking at the door and crying, not that they would be unclothed but clothed upon, that their morality might be swallowed up of life. Christopher Morley, in one of his delightful essays, running on about the man whose business it is to write, describes the process:

He spreads out the various lines of tension in his mind precisely as a spider builds his web, his web of expectation, not knowing exactly what he is going to write or exactly what is going to happen; only knowing, just as the spider knows, that something will fly into that web, and he himself will be surprised. You get a certain feeling, a notion of some idea. . . . You jot down or try to fix the picture . . . and spend weeks or months . . . before anything happens. Then something falls into the web.[8]

And there will be no dearth, gentlemen, for the man who keeps his web spread out widely and in good repair.

The very hardest thinking [says John Oman, quoting from Goethe] may not bring thoughts. They must come like good children of God and cry, "Here we are." Yet neither do they come unsought. You try your hardest. Then, after you have given up, they come sauntering in with their hands in their pockets, though if the effort had not opened the door to them they would not have come.[9]

Spells of hard thinking with the mind under full steam, followed by brief periods of incubation, even of idleness, when the conscious mind is relatively unoccupied, is, I dare say, as near a formula for fertility as a man can come.

But let us not exalt unduly this aspect of the minister's preparation. There is another great source from which his preaching will draw: his knowledge of human need, as he finds that need in his own heart and in the lives of his people. *Discharge all*

Your Duties as a Minister

writes Paul to Timothy (II Timothy 4:5). Sermons spring out of parishes too that are well tilled! In his quaint and homely fashion Gustave Frenssen writes of himself:

I usually choose my text in the evening, and turn it over in my mind. First of all I take the text out of its ancient setting and plant it in our own life, and in our own time. My text, so to speak, saunters up and down the village street once or twice with thoughtful eyes and meditative mind. It becomes accustomed to the village, learns to feel at home in it. Next morning I set to work in earnest. I work, as it were, in my shirt sleeves. Like a swift runner, I warm up to my work, and, as I write, I deliberately address certain definite people: Farmer L., Dr. M., P. the workman. . . . And so I feel that my sermons are firmly rooted in actual life, that each of them has a certain amount of strength, a certain power to quicken and inspire.[10]

So in the quieter moments of the day, which somehow you must secure for yourselves and guard, you are to brood upon life, its meaning, its purpose, its eternal values. Pass them in review as you read again the lessons for the coming Sunday: first your own life; then the life that in the homes of your congregation keeps tugging at your sleeve, or running off alone to weep, or breaking out in bitter resentments. Sermons, like books, are "good" only when "they meet some human hunger or refute some human error."[11] The man who knows men and has compassion on them will not be announcing the kind of theme one so often comes across in the columns of the press on Saturday morning, strange and fantastic bits of truth or near-truth, novelties (I Timothy 1:4-7), picked up from what odd corners. New, yes. As new as the wares of the boy who comes hawking his way through the commuters' train: "All the latest magazines and novels. Next week's current events straight from the press!" And you wonder if any of it will be as good tomorrow as it is today.

Charles Kingsley used to lean from his pulpit and say earnestly and solemnly to his people in the village church at Eversley, "Here we are again to talk about what is really going on in your soul and mine." Do that yourself, if not in the pulpit then in the study; and you will not be preaching what would have spoiled if you had let it stand twenty-four hours in the sun. Rather will you be facing each week, as Dr. Fosdick has said, some difficulty that men and women of flesh and blood, whose names you know, find starkly across the road, some question that folk seem to go on asking forever, some sin that fastens itself to their days, some mistaken judgment, some forgotten wealth. Then deeply pondering these things, you will bring to bear upon them the challenge and the sureness of God. What is it that will move Farmer L. and Dr. M. where they are, and after that give them power and peace? What is it that will stir a tumult in their souls and then compose it? Which is the best definition I know of any art. What would they "wish to have settled before they die?"[12] Dr. Henry Sloan Coffin once suggested that we ask these questions:

What ranges of Christian experience seem unknown to this congregation?

To what Christian principles do they appear blind?

What spiritual needs seem unmet?

What areas of individual and social life in this community seem to lie outside Christ's Kingdom?

What is lacking or defective in the Church's effect on the community?

What Christian resources are nominally listed by this congregation but not used?

What aspects of the Gospel have most immediate appeal to those not yet Christians?[13]

So, as you dwell not only upon themes but upon people, not so much upon ideas as upon life, does God's truth begin to stand up in your soul and beckon. You see its sweeping gesture in the very topics, as you leaf through a volume of Phillips Brooks' sermons: The Law of Growth, The Holiness of Duty, The Power of an Uncertain Future, Christ Our Life, The Mind's Love for God. These glowing, poignant ministries to the joy and travail of the human soul are not here today and gone tomorrow. They have dimensions and an abiding significance, because they link the horizons of our life with eternity. They speak to an age in the name of the ages and of God. We are bound at least to attempt it, every man in his day. Certainly one can never grow weary of trying. Themes like The Eagerness of God, The Silences of God, The Balances of God, The Vigor of the Gospel, The Pale Galilean, Our Footing on the Heights, What are you Making of Life?, New Lives for Old, Flying Colors. Whatever we may or may not be able to do with them subsequently, we can manage to aim anyhow in the direction of matters that to the needy lives of men are not peripheral. We can have a kind of wishful fling at central and momentous things. We can leave off the hurried sewing together of old scraps or new and bend our backs, even though more often than not we bend them in vain, to weave some garment of "power and distinction," knowing that the pattern for our weaving is to be found in the pages of no book. It is to be found there among the hills toward which we shall keep lifting our eyes as we walk with man, and men, and a Man through the valley of many shadows, beside the still waters.

So much for the kind of preparation that is lifelong, the spade work from which alone full harvests grow. But each week, as you

### Set Your Heart on Prophecy*

there is a kind
of preparation which has to point itself, so to speak, into a very
particular and crucial process. That specific pointing up toward
the sermon should begin, I submit, on Monday morning. I am
no great believer in the blue-Monday theory, and the dominie's
ineffable exhaustion, physically and spiritually, after the ardu-
ous labors of Sunday. Sunday will exhilarate a healthy man who
loves his work. It is the climax of the week, and a refreshment
to the soul that has toiled faithfully to its summit. There may
be a certain amount of normal reaction on Sunday evening
about nine o'clock. I have always enjoyed then more than at
any other time an hour or two with friends, particularly if I
myself have conducted the second service. But by Monday
morning a healthy man should start tightening his knapsack
again for the climb. Or, to put it differently, he should be feeling once more the initial thrill of the hunt. If you simply must
play golf, all right, go ahead; but consider the afternoon, how
long it is, and postpone the game. Get started first on the quest.

Shall we say that you have had now your own private morning devotions? When you turn to your desk, it may be that
some theme is already knocking imperiously at the door of
your mind. Or you may even have outlined a course of sermons,
as I have done, six months in advance. I used to think it could
be managed in no such cold blood. But it can. If you have not
determined on anything beforehand, you begin at the beginning.

First of all, should you belong to one of the so-called litur-
gical groups, you read the lessons appointed for the next Sunday. In lieu of them let me plead with you to follow through
the year some plan of your own and not just haphazardly to
fasten on whatever comes to you, even after praying about it.

* I Corinthians 14:1.

I was told once, when I inquired what was wanted of me in a certain series of services, to get the answer on my knees. May I say quite reverently that most answers for me seem to come when I am wearing out the rug in my study, walking up and down, or the seat of my trousers as I squirm about at my desk? What Paul says to Timothy, his lawful son in the faith, seems to provide me with some justification:

Attend to Your Scripture-reading

*your preaching,*

*your teaching. . . . You have a gift. . . . Do not neglect* it. So will you *save your hearers as well as yourself* (I Timothy 4:13, 14, 16).

I would encourage you to spend as much as an hour or two going over the passages provided you by the appointed lessons, or such as you have allotted yourself, letting them sink deeply into your thought, setting down some sudden flash of light from another facet of the truth you had never seen before, allowing sentence after sentence to lie quietly in your mind until it begins to speak. For almost twenty-five years now I have done most of my morning preaching on the pericopes (or, as a printer once suffered the word to stand, the "periscopes!"), those selections of epistle and gospel worked out for all the Sundays of the church year with an eye to the whole round content of the Christian faith; and I have never felt them to be a hindrance or a slavery. It has been one of the most amazing facts of my experience to find opening through them one avenue after another, vista upon vista. Nothing else has so persuaded me that these familiar words of Scripture hold enshrined within them the inexhaustible riches of God.

Take only by way of illustration the third chapter of the fourth gospel, from which, in the Authorized Version, is taken for Trinity Sunday the story of Nicodemus. You should never be bored by Nicodemus, from this shadowed hour on the housetop to that other when with Joseph of Arimathea he boldly brought his ointment to the tomb. Of him, with his little concealments, his wistful hesitations, his agonizing uncertainties, you may find yourself speaking on a day under some such topic as One Man Against Himself: held back by his own position in Jerusalem, held back by what others thought, held back by the risks of discipleship; all these pulling one way, and Christ and many an old dream pulling the other. There is a sermon somewhere there. You have met that man. You *are* that man!

Another day, poring over the same story, you are brought up sharp, as if for the first time, by the quick demand with which Christ breaks into that other's all too timid acknowledgment of him as a kind of rabbi: *Verily, verily, I say unto thee, except a man be born again, he cannot see the kingdom of God.* And you think, it may be, of those lines from Emerson:

> Heartily know
> When half-gods go
> The gods arrive.

Or again, there is that weird sound of the wind, blowing *where it listeth,* and ye cannot tell *whence it cometh* or *whither it goeth.* One may wish to preach now on Life as Mystery. And surely, sooner or later, and again and again, on that "gospel in miniature," as Luther called it: *For God so loved the world that he gave his only begotten Son, that whosoever believeth in him should not perish, but have everlasting life.* Do not side-step that. It is too big for you. It is too big for all of us. But tackle it. Stand under the shadow of it. You will grow taller there and wear an added dignity. People do who live at the foot of Everest or the Matterhorn. Throw down your glove in front of such a glory half a dozen times a year, for your own soul's stature if for nothing else. Gaze out across those majestic heights and their great, still beauty. Make for their arresting slopes and that companionable air. And once more as of old, *the spirit of man* shall be as *the candle of the Lord* (Proverbs 20:27, A.V.).

But let us say, for we mean to sweat about this thing, that still no theme stands compellingly before your face, to gather up the threads of your vacant thought. What then? Why, then,

Watch Yourself and Watch Your Teaching*

Frequently,

and I judge that I am to set down here my own experience, I leaf back through my latest manuscript book of sermons, for instance, to see in a kind of perspective what I have preached about over the period of the last six months; or it may even be a year. And as I think of the lives of my people, and of the great, stirring trends becoming so obvious in the life of mankind, out of my very omissions and silences springs now and then the consciousness of needs that I have not even tried to meet, of truths clamoring for their share of recognition. However elaborate our creed, says James Reid, the things we live by are very few. I dare say offhand there are no more than fifty, if that many, pivotal truths in the whole sweep of the gospel. Set them down some time for yourself: The Nature of Man, The Greatness of God, The Meaning of Life, The Fact of Sin, The Mysteries of the Cross, The Power of the Spirit, The Destiny of the Human Soul, and so on. List them; and if you are ever at a loss for a subject, go back and see which of them you have been side-stepping. Then make your choice, not so much of something you want to do perhaps, as of something you ought to do.

However, for our purpose here, we shall not let that work either. Then I suggest that you leaf through some other man's sermons for an hour: Gossip's, Hutton's, Buttrick's, Fosdick's, Sockman's, Farmer's, Stewart's, Reid's. Give them a chance to make your kettle boil. I do wish that Burnet's were available. You do not need to be captivated by them and led off nose first to say what they said. You can be kindled by them. Hough has

* I Timothy 4:16.

done that for me, besides these others that I have mentioned, and Stanley Jones, and Leslie Weatherhead, and Reinhold Niebuhr, not to mention the preacher's perennial help, Halford Luccock! I am not talking now of plagiarism; I am talking of ideas, born of other ideas, and giving birth to your own in turn. They will belong finally to him who provides them with the best expression.

Oman tells of the old Irish minister who had been consulted on this matter by a younger brother. And he answered, "Well, you remember about the priest's portion in the Old Testament?" "No," said the younger, who had forgotten if he ever remembered. "Why," went on the other, "he stuck his fork into the pot and whatever stuck to it was his." (I Samuel 2:13, 14)

> When 'Omer smote 'is bloomin' lyre,
> 'E'd 'eard men sing by land and sea,
> An' what 'e thought 'e might require,
> 'E went and took, the same as me.
>
> They knew 'e stole, 'e knew they know'd,
> They didn't talk nor make a fuss
> But winked at 'Omer down the road,
> And 'e winked back, the same as us.

"When you make as good use of it as Homer," adds Dr. Oman, "and do it as openly, you can annex as much as you like and approve yourself for doing it."[14] No one need be ashamed of that give and take. Frederick Robertson of Brighton used to declare that he could never "light his own fire."[15] No man's labor was a substitute for his, but any man's insight he would unhesitatingly lay under tribute to his own.

Only, whatever you do, do not throw it all over that Monday morning and let it go and hope that by Tuesday an inspiration will come. As the old Scot's Golf Manual says, according to Adam Burnet: "Never gie in, your opponent micht dee!" Have at it and stick at it. Walk a mile in the middle of it if you must, though I would say only under the severest provocation, if your brain is full of cobwebs and stale odors. But come back. If nothing grips you, shut your teeth and do the gripping yourself. I have wasted more time than I care to record waiting for the divine spirit to move upon the water. Jesus once said to ten sadly afflicted men, "Go and show yourselves to the priests"; and as they went they were cleansed. You get hold of a subject sometimes simply by choosing it, instead of sitting around vaguely if hopefully on the off-chance that a subject will choose you. You should be uneasy, perhaps even by Monday noon, or on the direst occasions by Tuesday at the latest, if you do not have your theme for the coming Sunday safely in hand, clearly and succinctly stated for the bulletin, and frequently summed up in two or three pointed sentences designed to arrest attention and to arouse some interest.

When that is done, you have the satisfaction of knowing that a real start has been made. The selection of a theme sets a man his objective; its early selection and his early struggle with it enables him to let it simmer a while down somewhere in the subconscious, percolate now and then, and so rid itself of its most distressing crudities. Its announcement shuts off all speculation among his people as to whether or not he decides on Saturday night what he is going to preach about on Sunday morning. Already, with a dawning knowledge of what it is he wants to accomplish, and with more than a dawning knowledge of what his text really means (for, mind you, he has by this time gone into that with great care), having now several aspects of his proposition or problem opened up in the brief sentences he has used to advertise it, his sermon almost insensibly has begun to take on a certain form. And unless he transgresses shamelessly the grounds that are set, it has achieved even at this point a certain unity.

The next step, I suppose, if you mean to be among other things

### A Skilled Teacher*

is to determine what kind of sermon you purpose to preach. I know you cannot dissect a living process and keep it alive. I know you cannot reduce creative activity to a timetable. But along here somewhere, and just about now, you have to fix the general trend of things. You are familiar with the different types of sermon: doctrinal, expository, ethical, pastoral, evangelistic. Let me only say again that I have never preached or heard or read a sermon worthy of the name which was not to a greater or less degree all five of these together, precisely as a good novel is made up of narrative, description, characterization, and dialogue. *Even the body consists not of one member but of many. . . . The eye cannot say to the hand, I have no need of you, nor again the head to the feet, I have no need of you. . . . If the body were all eye, where would hearing be? If the body were all ear, where would smell be? . . . God has tempered the body together.* (I Corinthians 12:14, 21, 17, 24) We would better see to it that the sermon is too. A sermon without exposition, with nothing which leads to a clearer understanding of God's Word, is without its highest sanction. A sermon without doctrine, with nothing which leads to a clearer understanding of the cardinal tenets of the Christian faith, is without foundation. A sermon without the ethical is pointless. The story is told of a young preacher who after announcing his text began, "I dare say you are afraid that these words forecast a practical sermon; let me assure you that you will not find it so!"[16] A sermon without the pastoral is spiritless. And a sermon without the evangelistic is Christless and useless altogether!

It may well be, however, that the emphasis should vary from week to week. Indeed, my advice is that you deliberately vary it. Determine that next Sunday you will have to do chiefly with

* II Timothy 2:24.

exposition. Only remember, you who are unwisely inclined to carry your historical and critical moods into the pulpit with you, that it is to be an exposition, and not an exposé! C. S. Lewis has a shrewd hit at the so-called "historical point of view":

Put briefly, it means that when a learned man is presented with any statement by an ancient author, the one question he never asks is whether it is true. He asks who influenced the ancient writer, and how far the statement is consistent with what he said in other books, and what phase in the writer's development, or in the general history of thought, it illustrates, and how it affected other writers, and how often it has been misunderstood (specially by the learned man's own colleagues), and what the general course of criticism has been on it for the last ten years, and what is the present state of the question. To regard the ancient writer as a possible source of knowledge . . . would be rejected as unutterably simple-minded. . . . And so, thanks to . . . the historical point of view, great scholars are now as little nourished by the past as the most ignorant mechanic who holds that "history is bunk."[17]

Scripture is to be expounded—that *open secret of the gospel* (Ephesians 6:19) fully and freely—not exposed. And please do let it get you somewhere, like that old, old sermon on the Prodigal with its indelible divisions, Sick of Home, Home-sick, Home.[18] Let it get you as that does into some gallant article of the Christian faith, and out of that into a radiant life, as followers of Jesus Christ and workers together with God. The Sunday after, take a doctrine; but do not on that account suppose you are free to shake off with a rude and impatient hand this Scripture that was written for our learning. There is room for the Word of God even in doctrinal sermons. And do not turn your back on the workaday world where men are to have their fling at living what you say! Ethics is nothing but doctrine gone off on an errand. The Sermon on the Mount is the Lord's Prayer in overalls. And whatever you say, may it be said in the name and fellowship of Him Who is the Head of His

body, the church; even as we are *severally members of it*—
(I Corinthians 12:27).

After you have determined what emphasis your subject and
material call for, it is then that you begin to organize your
thought under heads. And I am definitely of the opinion that
it is well for the structure to show. There is no painting the
human figure without some knowledge of human anatomy;
and unless the framework is manifest to a degree, what you
have is no longer human. It is either surrealism or it is a jelly-
fish. I have listened to sermons that without aim did "go round,"
as Browning has it, "in an eddy of purposeless dust, effort unending and vain." And I have preached them, too. The technique is not difficult. Like an Englishman at his bath, you
plunge right in and splash around a bit.[19] Having nothing to
say which has seemed to you of sufficient importance to compel a clear analysis, you fill in the necessary time with a few remarks. You aim at nothing in particular, and hit it squarely in
the middle.[20] The only sane question a hearer can ask when it is
over is, What on earth was it all about? And the only sane answer anyone can give is, About everything. On nothing. You
are to have a framework—and let it show—making no vulgar
display of it, as if your skeleton were exhibit A, Victim of Famine in the Ukraine; yet not allowing what you are supposed to
have in hand wander hazily abroad like an indeterminate fog.

The divisions may be two or three in number, rarely more.
There is, of course, no magic formula. One of my professors
used to insist on an unwavering three, because a twig divides
into three as a rule; and all this had something to do with the
Trinity! I was positively superstitious about it at first. It was
profoundly important. So you hustled around until you found
not two, not four, but three. Later you discover that logic, in the
phrase of Dr. Fosdick, has more to do with the thing than
magic; and psychology, more than metaphysics.

Now and then the decision is made for you. There are times when a text will fall wide open into its inevitable parts and offer you a present of its own internal arrangements. I am reminded at the moment of such a text. I have already referred to it. On a memorable day it gave me one look, split itself into thirds, and lay down on my paper. It was the third and fourth and fifth verses of the thirteenth chapter of John: *Knowing that he had come from God and was going to God, he . . . tied a towel round him, . . . and began to wash the feet of the disciples. Knowing that he had come from God.* What is the origin of life? *And was going to God.* What is its goal? *He tied a towel round him.* How therefore shall life occupy itself between? And the theme was, Why Are We Here? The sermon which was preached that next Sunday was not custommade. It came ready-to-wear! Perhaps it is not necessary to say that you will likely enough be able to count such occasions on the fingers of two hands.

Once in a while, instead of beginning with it, a preacher will want to end with the text. He plans not to start out with something given but to arrive at something discovered. In this case the divisions will follow each other in a logical or psychological sequence, moving in a straight line, like the links of a chain. Not after the fashion of a detective story, where Truth plays the role of the murderer and nobody can even begin to guess its whereabouts until the last page! We are not in the pulpit to keep people in suspense or to darken their minds with mystery. But let me illustrate what I mean.

Suppose we take some such theme as Strength Made Perfect in Weakness (II Corinthians 12:9), the answer Paul got when he prayed about his thorn: *It is in weakness that my power is fully felt.* You begin back of your text somewhere with the suggestion, and surely it can be driven well home, that the world is too strong for us. Then you mark the power of God, how unobstrusive it is for the most part: the growth of flowers, the silent orbit of the stars, the long patience of His love. Until at last you understand that Christ is not asking of you or of me or of anybody else strength. Our ideas of strength are not like His. He is asking of us a clear passage through our self-esteem for the power that makes itself fully felt only when we have learned to distrust our own. He is asking us to stand with God under our feet to be men on! So do we come up with the text!

Or again, as you brood over some Scripture, unraveling the lines of its thought, pulling them apart and weaving them into one again, the divisions may appear as co-ordinate strands, each rendering its own support to the central theme. Once more by way of illustration, here is a sermon—shall we say—on the subject, Jesus Christ and the Middle-Class Mind, in which one purposes to disclose the hidden perils that lurk in our democratic psychology. They are the very perils that go stalking about Jesus as he enters Jerusalem in triumph. The doctrine of equality, in accordance with which everybody is on a level with everybody else, and the hut periodically tears down the palace, and the gutter stones the saint! The second peril is that worshipful doctrine of rugged individualism, so dear to all folk who do not choose to be controlled in the public interest, but prefer to look out for their own and do it first. The third will be the doctrine of the majority vote: the voice of the people, so strangely unlike the voice of God, calling for Barabbas, hounding a silent Figure up a little hill toward a cross. Thank God, then, that in His heart there is a Kingdom, with shining dignities for a soul to grow in. You do not have to do what they did back in 1770 with the prayer-book of the old Bruton Parish Church in Williamsburg: run a line through Kingdom and write in The Republic of Heaven; strike out King of Kings and leave only Lord of Lords. There is an aristocracy of spiritual stature. In a world like ours with its bourgeois ideology, Jesus of Nazareth lost his life!

Once we have got the main heads of our discourse clearly in

mind, their relationships and sequences clearly indicated, the points arranged in the most telling order, without overlapping, driving on toward some great truth or obligation, for always man's only peace lies in his acceptance of a challenge, then it is time to block out the introduction and the conclusion. Not before, lest the introduction fail to introduce, and the conclusion fall short of concluding.

Hugh Black, formerly of Union, used to insist that there was but one proper way in which to introduce a sermon, and that was by giving the text its setting in the context and in history, showing it against its background of thought and incident. Frequently such a procedure is highly desirable; sometimes it is unavoidable. But it is not necessary to forge an iron-bound rule out of it. Maybe it is not the text that needs introducing anyway. It may be the audience.

You may begin therefore in any one of a number of ways; remembering only that if you are too brilliant, you will not live up to it, and if you are too heavy, you will never live it down or preach it up. You may begin with an apt story or pertinent quotation. I remember coming across a suggestion for an opening sentence on Life to the Full,[21] and using it. It was that cutting cynicism of Synge, with which some of you may be familiar: "Life is a table d'hôte in a rather dirty restaurant, with time changing the plates before you have had enough to eat." I went back to look at that sermon again as I wrote this. The introduction seems to me now like a blitzkrieg that did not quite come off.

Or you may begin with the high light of some contrast. One university preacher is said to have quoted as his text at chapel Hazael's words to Elisha: *Is thy servant a dog, that he should do this thing?* (II Kings 8:13, A.V.) He then looked up and said, "Well, dog or no dog, he did it." They tell me the students listened that day. Unfortunately the passage means no such thing. Perhaps it would be better to preach on a text that is really there, even though it be not so interesting.

Of course, the disadvantage with all such muscular suddenness is that it tends to throw the sermon off balance at the
start and raise a titter. It is said that some critic complained
about a young novelist's book, telling him he was far too tedious
in getting off, that the very first sentence should plunge one *in
medias res*. So the lad cut the whole opening chapter of his
manuscript and substituted this: " 'Dammit, no!' said the duch-
ess, who up to this time had taken no part in the conversation."

Occasionally one may wish to start with a striking similarity,
or with a clearing away of underbrush, or with some current
situation. Here is Gustav Frenssen beginning a sermon on
Peter:

This is the season in which nature does not know her mind. In
the daytime the wind is warm. . . . Yet when the sun sets it grows
very cold. In the daytime the sun smiles on us. . . . At night comes
the wind, as though he were some stern preacher sent to rebuke
us for our sins. . . . There is ceaseless change. The old will not
go and the new will not come.

Now, most men are like that. They are like the weather . . .
'twixt spring and winter; they are changeable as March. They
think of their sorrows and they are afraid; then they remember
their sins and laugh. Now they look backwards and their hearts
fail them; now they look forward with concern. One day they
repent; the next they make good resolutions; the day after, they
are quite indifferent once more. They go round and round in a
circle like that old horse of yours which drives your threshing
mill. . . . In one passage the Gospel tells

of such a man.

Then comes the announcement of the text, Mark 14:66–72.

Only in any case, and in every case, be sure that the introduction is an introduction, the function of which is not simply to
arouse interest but to introduce. No more, no less. Above all, it
must be relevant and not make people begin to wonder, "For
heaven's sake what's he driving at now?" That is a bad start al-

ways. Let it bring them to understand that something real and pressing is afoot. With deliberate violence, not so much of manner as of matter, let it seize their restful minds, before they settle back for one more sermon, out of the past tense into which Scripture so often seems to throw people quite unaccountably, and snatch them away into a realization that it is not the there and then with which you have to deal but the here and now. If the theme, for instance, be our Sin of Esau, a few swift strokes will be enough to recall the story: whereupon straightway may be lifted out of the contemporary scheme the disposition of our modern world to throw overboard as Esau did many of its most precious birthrights; at least to sneer at them and reckon them of less worth than a stomach full.

When it seems advisable to give the historical background, bring to it all the consecrated imagination you can muster. Reconstitute, re-people, re-create that ancient world as best you can. Writes Jowett:

Catch the sounds and secrets in the air, touch the hurrying people, nod to the shepherd on the hills. Go with Amos to Bethel, and note the very things he sees along the road. Go with Hosea. . . . Look into the houses and workshops.[22]

In no other way can you make it come alive.

Shall we say you want to preach on The Ultimate Secret of the Good Life? And you want everyone to see that it is not obedience, and it is not loyalty; you have discovered that it is a kind of uncalculating gallantry. Your text is Matthew 21:8— *And a very great multitude spread their garments in the way* (A.V.). You begin: "There have been heroic figures that many a city in our own time has welcomed in some such fashion as that, though instead of garments and branches we use telephone directories and ticker tape. But there is the same abandon about it all, the same refreshing recklessness as the spirit of man lets itself go, leaving all its net balances and figures at home in the ledger, snatching off its coat, throwing its hat in the air, and tossing on the road any token of devotion it can get its hand on. Others may tidy up and count the cost after, if that is their mood!" So you come to speak of the love that "forgets itself into immortality."

Perhaps I may be forgiven another illustration. Remember, we are trying to bring some Scripture that is "superbly out of date" and set it down in the modern world as if it were quite at home. The text is Amos 5:18: *The day of the Lord is darkness, and not light.* You begin: "He was talking to people who were altogether too sure of God. They could not conceive it possible that instead of being for them God might be against them. The king, and even history itself, had done an all-round good job for the moment of making at least the better people quite comfortable. Most of them, it is true, were far too rich for their own use or anybody's else. Many of them were amazingly callous, so that you did not stand a great chance of having any justice done you anywhere unless you had a bit of pull. There was not much genuine morality left even in religion. The most outrageous things went on under the cloak of piety. When suddenly this simple herdsman and fruit-grower, from an altogether different section of the country, came up North,—to New York from Alabama!—and began to fling his thunderbolts around. You can imagine how popular he was. He said it would not do, not any of it. God was still in the picture, and God was not playing their game. The day of the Lord was about to dawn, and it was darkness, not light. Of course, nobody paid any attention; nobody but history itself. Everybody knew whose side God was on, until history gave the lie to it. They had almost half a century yet in Israel before they were destroyed!"

And you go on to speak of the God who reveals Himself in the inevitability of His moral order.

I say, whatever you do when you get on your feet, breathe the breath of life into the stuff you have taken in your hands. Do not let it lie there like a lump, dead and inert. Somewhere in one of his prefaces, Robert Louis Stevenson gives as his counsel to every author, "What he cannot vivify, he should omit."[23]

But equally important with the introduction is the conclusion. Many of us make splendid approach shots and lose the hole after we get on the green. And many a horse is numbered an "also ran" because the jockey did not save anything for the finish! It need not be long, the conclusion. It should not be long. Let it summarize, if you will, in a brief, pungent, telling paragraph the chief heads of your sermon, restating them perhaps and showing their organic relation to the one great whole of your text. Or let it bring home to your hearers all at once, gathering their thought to a sharp focus, some final, practical, and pointed application. Or let us say that you have planned to leave them quietly in love and awe at the feet of Jesus, there being nowhere else to go at the end of a sermon.

If words seem recalcitrant, unwilling to lend themselves to the burden of reality that weighs upon your spirit, tell a story. Practice telling stories, perhaps some day to your children. You will never be able to interest them with things that are dull as dish-water. Nothing dull has any place in their lives. Perhaps that way you may learn to tell a story well, even in the pulpit. I remember not long ago straining to find something that would carry conviction on the matter of how a man could get out of his own way. It seemed to me that better than anything else that day my people should be able to watch it going on. There was Thomas Kelly, in his *Testament of Devotion;* but so much of it struck my mood as being too mystical and far away. When all at once Simon, son of Jona, came to my rescue: stumbling around from insight to denial, from dear intimacy to the dark, where he wept so bitterly. Then you hear his feet running toward an empty tomb; and you watch him the day he flung off his fisherman's cloak, leaped into the water and swam toward the radiant figure on the beach,—with nothing left that mat-

tered now, except the whole round earth that Jesus had "torn
out of his heart only to fling it back," that they might carry it
together through the years in "an infinite tenderness." It was
Peter at last, and not Simon. A sermon could stop there.[24]

Or better by far the way Dean Sperry of Harvard did it one
Sunday in the chapel of the University of Chicago. He had
begun with a vivid account of Albert Schweitzer and closed
with the day that scholar, musician, medical missionary, was
fashioning a log for his hospital. A native who stood looking
on was asked to help, but said he could not very well because
he was an intellectual. Answered the modern saint, "I thought
I was an intellectual once," and chipped away quietly at the log.

But whatever your purpose, however you arrange it, let the
closing sentences clinch the matter,—lest half-a-dozen good
things, or things not half so good, be left hanging in the air with
no visible means of support. One preacher of my acquaintance,
who be it said is never ordinary, seems simply to look at his
watch, complete the current thought, and sit down, leaving
most people breathless and just a little embarrassed for the
choir, unprepared as they are to bring to any timely birth the
proper response. I grant you, his method is no end better than
the inability to put a sermon down under which some men
labor. They make you think of a baker with sticky dough on
his hands. They just cannot get rid of it.

But surely there is a mean somewhere between extremes. One
should stop, yet do more than stop: one should finish, with a
little finish. There is no need to turn loose the fountains of eloquence, as the old rhetoricians used to advise. What is done
should be done simply and quietly. But it should leave no doubt
as to the solemn duty or the high faith or the royal privilege toward which all that you have said has been pressing your hearers so steadily, as you would press back a crowd, until you have
shut them up to God in Christ, and to the cleansing, healing,
holding power of His eternal Spirit.

❧ ❧

Ah, but a man's reach should exceed his grasp,
Or what's a heaven for?
                    ROBERT BROWNING, "Andrea del Sarto"

✓✓✓✓✓✓✓✓✓✓✓✓✓✓✓✓✓✓✓✓✓✓✓✓✓✓✓✓✓✓✓✓✓✓✓✓✓✓✓✓✓✓✓✓

# Chapter 6

## THE WAY YOU HANDLE THE WORD OF TRUTH*

✓✓✓✓✓✓✓✓✓✓✓✓✓✓✓✓✓✓✓✓✓✓✓✓✓✓✓✓✓✓✓✓✓✓✓✓✓✓✓✓✓✓✓✓

It is to be understood that by this time we have the framework
of the sermon entire. The introduction, the divisions and sub-
divisions, and the conclusion have been blocked out in pencil
first, on a sizable sheet of paper; to be copied later in ink, perhaps on the page of some notebook which you plan to keep,
a full and revised outline to guide your writing. One cannot
always be sure of sticking closely by it. There are times when
your mind, set finally to its task, will take the bit in its teeth
and go off so to speak on its own. If it is not bent on making a
fool of itself, follow it. It may know what to do better than you,
having worked at it when you were not looking. But if it shows
signs of running out of liberty into license, check it with a
rough hand.

Meanwhile, and for the moment, it might be well for you to
* II Timothy 2:15.

remember that you are not necessarily preparing anything for posterity. I have often found in this realization a certain freedom and release from the particular embarrassments of that eighteenth century preacher who, it was said, took so long to dress his sermons that they caught cold.[1] You have already made, of course, a thorough exegetical study of your text and have *full insight into its meaning* (I Corinthians 1:5). We have been more or less taking that for granted. There is very little value to be had from preaching on a text that is not there! You begin next to mull over point by point, ready to set down instantly any thought that occurs to you, assigning it its proper place in the scheme. If at first glance it seems irrelevant, squeeze it in somewhere, perhaps along the right-hand margin, for more mature and leisurely consideration. But get it on paper, relevant or irrelevant. You may be surprised at what these things jotted down here at the side will do to your sermon in the end.

As you think you way around and in and out, the titles of books may occur to you, books dealing with the same or with some kindred subject—a sentence, it may be from a novel, bits of poetry, incidents: get every one of them down. Then go and page through the books; read the scenes again, and the poetry, though I should use the poetry sparingly. Enter what you have under its appropriate head on your paper. Consult your own book of commonplaces for illustrations and suggestions. Keep your hands off *The Preacher's Manual!* Read other sermons if you remember any on this theme which have really stirred you. Maintain between the parts, in length and in content, as reasonable a balance as you can. And almost as important as anything else, get all this done promptly enough to leave you a little time for the kind of brooding a man can do as he goes about his other tasks. Ideas will flash across your inner darkness when you are least expecting them. You may be on a subway platform, as I was once when a sermon leaped at me out of somewhere (pardon me this immodesty) as Minerva burst from the brain of Jove. It would have been too bad if I had left my pen and notebook at home! Things really do happen if after organizing your material you can let it stand awhile, sleep over it perhaps—I mean at night—and give that mysterious self of yours which dwells beneath the surface of your conscious life a chance, kindly if it will, peevishly if it must, to throw something at you out of the cellar.

Not later than Thursday morning if you can possibly manage it, you begin to write. And let me say this again, this time with violence: I would not give a brass farthing, as a rule, for a preacher who does not write at least one sermon a week for the first ten or fifteen years of his ministry. It is a discipline that no man can afford to forego. To write only the first half and leave the second half to God, as one young preacher said was his habit, merely exposes you to the compliment that was paid him: "Sir," remarked his monitor, "I congratulate you indeed! Your half is unfailingly better than God's!"

There may be times when on Friday or Saturday a sermon other than that which you have written will lay compelling hands on you and drive you into the pulpit with no shred of a manuscript either in front of you or behind you. Or a week may come tearing along through your life, driving you hither and yon, giving you no chance to write. Very good. Then preach as you can, and be unashamed. Do not begin, as I heard a man begin under such circumstances, by apologizing for not being prepared. The congregation will likely enough find that out before you get very far! Just leave them to their own devices and do the best you know how. Happy, then, the preacher who can fall back on years of faithful work, whose mind is accustomed to control!

But the kind of pious palaver which older and more experienced ministers sometimes give the younger about not having every sentence rounded out and polished too prettily, about being altogether too careful and too precise, about throwing oneself on the mercy of God and saying what is in one's heart: to me that is an abomination, and it is wicked. You do not have to wait until Sunday morning to throw yourself on the mercy of God; you can do it the Monday before and have a few days in which to appropriate the mercy when it comes!

Write. And here again, make it a point every week to be through writing if you can by the evening of Friday, so that on Saturday you can go over it and revise it, rearrange it if necessary, maybe reduce it by one-third, as an editor once recommended with regard to some manuscript, and leave nothing out.[2] Roberts, the author of *Northwest Passage,* is said to have written first two million words and then cut it to three hundred thousand. One sermon written out each week with some workmanship—that is the rule.

And may I counsel you not to write the original draft in ink? There seems to be less finality about it when you do it in pencil, and as a result the words come more smoothly. You are free to express your mind without restraint if you are aware the while that it is all going to be worked over again anyhow. Especially will you find it easier to get started. I have spent hours, sometimes a whole morning, in front of my typewriter trying to get an opening sentence to satisfy me. The thing to do is to plunge in and promise yourself to come back and fix up everything that needs fixing. Hence the pencil. You can tear it all up if you like without so much hesitation and start entirely fresh. "Begin as poorly as you must," writes Dr. Hutton; "you can cut off the head later."[3] The same thing will keep happening in the body of the sermon. You will find yourself again and again stuck fast in the mire, trying to be effective. You will be trying to write better than you can. Then suddenly you say to yourself, "What's the use of fiddling about with this? I'll come back." And you are off. Hence the pencil.

Just do not quit; as in the preliminary work, so here. Stay with it. Change your position from the desk to a chair, with a writing board across your knees, from one room perhaps to an-other. Walk up and down. But keep at it. You will be inclined perhaps to look through the window at the sunshine and, hav-ing written no word for half an hour, to argue that you are all worn out. Your mind is not working; the inspiration is lacking somehow; it would be better to go and catch a fish. How it will be with you I cannot say. I am not often helped by such devices on the part of my soporific three-fourths to get by the other fourth, which never is much good as a sentry, until all of us can go to a movie! There is virtue in laying down the law to these recalcitrant selves inside of ours. If they will not agree to your schedule, you stage a sit-down. You say to them, "No work, no do anything else. Bide right here, today, tomor-row. We'll see who's who." It is amazing how docile and will-ing a servant the mind becomes finally when this little ques-tion of head-man-of-the-tribe is settled once and for all!

With regard to the actual writing, there is hardly an end to the suggestions one could offer. Perhaps the most essential thing is that you keep always before your mind's eye the people to whom you shall speak. Not that you are to introduce something here for this man's benefit, or something there which may have some particular bearing upon that woman and the way she acted at the congregational meeting; but you should visualize, while you write, as many living, needy, real people as you can, and say to them straightforwardly what is in your heart. The farther away you can get from embroidered essays on fascinat-ing fancies, the better; and the nearer you can get to the spirit and the manner of an earnest and private conversation, the more effective will your sermon become. *You are*

A Letter of Christ

*which I have been em-ployed to inscribe,* writes Paul to the Corinthians (II Corin-thians 3:3). That is precisely the view of the matter which I hope we may take as we face our congregations.

I do not for a moment mean to rule out any legitimate flight of the imagination or any useful passion. I mean to make everything subservient to one purpose, and that purpose not the writing of a great sermon or the elaboration of some mighty and puissant theme, but the ministering to human souls of the redemptive power of God. Do bear that forever in mind. Principal Denney used to say, "No man can give at once the impression that he himself is clever and that Christ is mighty to save." You are preaching not to make clear what good preaching is or ought to be; you are preaching to lay hold desperately on life, broken life, hurt life, soiled life, staggering life, helpless life, hard, cynical, indifferent, willful life, to lay hold on it with both hands in the high name of the Lord Christ and to lift it toward his dream.

By the same token it is necessary as you write to keep constantly at the fore your own prime function: as a prophet, in the commonly accepted sense of one who proclaims the will of God to the social order, no. Personally, I think the role of prophet can be overplayed. Your function as a teacher then? No. Not primarily. You are not, first of all, in the pulpit or at your desk as a specialist in religion, showing people how to do things, charting their course for them, pointing the way they should go. You are there as a religious personality, bearing witness to Christ and to the power of his presence and his peace. Write with that understanding.

If you have occasion to say "I," for pity's sake say it; and quit walking around on the stilts of some substitute. There is no need in modesty's cause to forego the honest impact of direct speech, that "I—thou" relationship on which Dr. Farmer lays such proper stress. The indefinite pronoun "one" seems particularly unhappy, with its long string of "ones" to follow like freight cars: One should think, if one thought, that one might not be able to find one's way through one's pronouns. It is about as effective as a wax phonograph record, broken. And that tall man at the circus, the editorial "we,"—the devil, whose name is Legion: "We would call your attention to the fifteenth verse of the second chapter of Hosea." You may be a large party like me; but you are not a crowd, and you are not fooling anybody. They know you mean "I." Of course, you do not have to stand that "I" in front of what you say so that no one can see or hear around it; but you do not need to dodge it all the time either, with some silly circumlocution. None but the self-conscious meek should do that. And they have their reward.

Remember, however, that it is not at all necessary for you to fill the whole sky from zenith to horizon with your own experiences. You may do it in lectures like these, but do not do it in the pulpit. I heard a forty-minute sermon some time ago that was not much of anything else. The preacher began with a few incidents which had marked the past week; and every time he made a point, he reached back in his knapsack for another incident. If nothing had happened to him that week we should not have had a sermon, and that might not have been so bad. Besides, among those who heard him, I dare say more than one could identify the people with whom those experiences had related him. And that comes uncomfortably near being a betrayal of confidence, an inexcusable pillorying of other men's private affairs. If I should ever recognize myself or some acquaintance in the story the minister told on Sunday, you may be sure I should not hurry to him again with anything I did not care to see become public property. A man does his people great injustice, and his own possible usefulness irreparable injury, when he begins to write unguardedly about the things that happen in his consultation room. I suppose it is possible to make use of them, certainly of the insights which they provide, but always with the utmost of caution.

Inasmuch as all such material drawn from experience or released from the consultation room is usually introduced by way of illustration, this may be as good a place as any in which to set down a few convictions with regard to that gentle art. Undoubtedly the first duty of an illustration is to illustrate. It should never itself take the place of thought and standing forth alone presume to offer the sermon its shoulders for a pickaback ride. To change the figure, you perhaps remember the fable of the mother frog who tried to puff herself to the size of that strange beast, a cow, which her offspring had seen in the meadow. "This big?" said she, swelling mightily. "Oh, much bigger, mother," came the answer. And so again and again to the point of inevitable dissolution. Well, a sermon can do that: blow itself up here with an anecdote, dilate itself yonder with a quotation, spread out somewhere else with a little distended rhetoric, until the strain on the few attenuated ideas in between grows too great and the whole thing simply bursts trying to get away from itself. My wife characterized a recent sermon of my own as being "six stories too high!"

Illustrations should illustrate, throw light and luster where it is needed; not like the incandescent suns they cart up in front of a movie set: you do not run off-stage and drag them in after any such fashion as that. They should be as natural to the context, as much in place, as unstudied and unobtrusive, as the glint of the moon on water. The most perfect examples are, of course, to be found in the parables of Jesus. There they are the simple, almost spontaneous response of an eager mind to the momentary stirring of the life around it. Someone has suggested that Jesus never produced a personal narrative or one of his own experiences.[4] To me that seems palpably untrue. It has long been a favorite thesis of mine that those eighteen hidden years in Nazareth were of all his years well-nigh the least hidden. I should like to think that on Christ's own lips they come alive. Lights spring up in the doorways of familiar homes; men and women move again along the lanes and highways of his youth. The laborers stand around from dawn to dusk in the public square waiting to be hired. Children pretend there is a wedding; and when they are tired of that they play "funeral." A sheep is lost one night in a storm. Hour after hour the shepherd thrusts his way along over the rocks and through the gullies, until at last it is safe in the fold again; and there is a knocking at doors and a shouting among friends above the noise of the wind. A coin is put away so carefully that it cannot be found; a woman takes a broom and sweeps the house by candlelight with the long, flickering shadows, and searches diligently while fantastic images dance about the walls. It may even be that her name is Mary. Over at the edge of the village lives a boy still who left one day for some far country across the hills; and the old father, heartsick, used to trudge down the lane at sunset night after night, as the years slipped by, to see if perchance a traveler might come wearily along whom he could recognize for a son—something about the fellow's walk or the set of the shoulders.

You can live over again the days when news came in from the world outside: about the wicked husbandman, away on the rough frontiers of Syria, who slew a landlord's son, as tenants have done many a time in Ireland; or the strong man armed, keeping his palace with all his goods in peace until a stronger than he came upon him and took from him his armor wherein he trusted and divided his spoils; about the owner who would build a tower and laid the foundations, but never counted the cost and could not finish it, so that people began pointing to it and laughing; or the merchant on the highway with his pearl; or the farmer with the treasure he had found. You can hear the whole village talking of such things in little knots at the street corner; while the commonplace lives of these commonplace people go on: bread rising behind the oven, a lamp on a stand, a meal-tub in the corner, a covey of birds, a sower scattering his seed, and always a lad whose thought keeps running out toward the Kingdom of God, listening, watching, then nodding to him-

self with some quick reference beyond, almost dazed to think
how much of forever is abroad today. Not once did he say to
anybody in later years, "Leave off now this staring at everything
around you and let me show you God."[5] Rather did he say,
"Don't look away; keep looking just there, until you see for
yourself how much of Forever is abroad today: this God,
Whose *invisible nature . . . and divine being,* since creation,
*have been quite perceptible in what He has made*" (Romans
1:20).

Natural, unstudied, unobtrusive: I wonder, in fact, if we may
not say that the illustration must not only illustrate the truth;
it must itself be that truth. Think of them in Paul: shadow-box-
ing and the race men run; a conquerer moving along the streets
of Rome; a vase talking back to the potter; the dispute between
the foot and the hand, the ear and the eye.[6] If your congregation
has to leave the main thread of your discourse, travel away to
something that was intended to illumine but has succeeded only
in distracting, then come back to the thought again—that always happens when you force the last good story you heard to
come in and do yeoman's service on Sunday morning under division II, subhead 1a, whether it fits or not; when your people
cannot quite get the point of your illustration, or get it ten minutes before you arrive at it, or like it so well that they sit down
inside of it with a chuckle and bring their lunch: in every such
event you have stultified your own purpose, utterly, devasta-
tingly. And the darkness is all the more intense for the light
that failed.

Certainly the most effective of all illustrations are the scenes,
the incidents, the stories, from Scripture, from fiction, from life,
that come most readily to a well-furnished mind, so readily
that they seem themselves to be integral parts in the movement
of the whole. They are not often to be had from books of so-
called illustrative matter, though no doubt at the beginning we
all use such first-aid kits; but in the end, nothing that is set

down there is really yours. That is the trouble with it: it is alien, it has not your spirit, it does not speak your language. Let me urge you to gather your own, if you must be a gleaner of them; index them as you go, if you have a bent for such methodical practice; better still, review them, appropriate them, get them somehow into your very system, so that they come running with a kind of inevitableness when your need of them is hardly conscious. That way and no other, by open-eyed awareness and the fixed habit of assimilation, on a day not too far distant, the dividends will begin trickling in. For a while it may be nothing more than a trickle; but things will improve. It is in this realm, too, that the rewards of diligence are most sure.

Now one of the foremost results of all the discipline which I have been trying so hard to describe and recommend is the achievement of a certain "style." There is a word for you that is often misunderstood. "Style" is not a mysterious something that you acquire only after years of laborious and painstaking effort; style is merely the way you have of expressing yourself. Your style may be good; it may be bad: but you have it already. You can change it for a better, or you can let it get altogether out of hand, if you like, and flop over into something that is worse. But you already have it. Improving it, strengthening it, beautifying it, pointing it, is no end of good sport. Forcing ideas to associate or come apart, bullying stubborn words to assume a certain pattern, all the fun, as someone has said, of being a dictator without any of the risks!

And it is not unworthy sport either. Surely the matter of what you say is most important; but the manner of your saying it runs a close second, whether you say it aptly or awkwardly, carelessly and cheaply, or with distinction. A sermon dare never be vulgar, as if the lost boy in the fifteenth chapter of Luke, to borrow John Oman's suggestion, had said: "I'd better get a move on and buzz along and pop in on my old dad and say,

'What about a new start, Governor?' " Yet it need not be polished either, as some men are, until it slips on its own polish.
Dr. Oman quotes one such on that same prodigal son, by way
of contrast:

I am determined to go to my dear, aged parent, and try to excite
his tenderness and compassion for me. I will kneel before him and
accost him in these penitent and pathetic terms: 'Best of parents!
I acknowledge myself an ungrateful creature to Heaven and to you.
Condescend to hire me into your family in the capacity of the
meanest slave.'[7]

This kind of Latinized eloquence is always a snare and a delu-
sion. Stay away from it. Anglo-Saxon roots grow sturdier trees.
They will provide you with all the useful excellence you need
and with sufficient nobility of expression to pay your debt to
God and man and your own soul, to the burden of divine pity
and human need.

My very first counsel then would be that you achieve a wholesome respect for words. Words are in themselves deeds. You
should study sometime the Old Testament conception of the
Word of God. The Word was God's act, it was His messenger,
His servant of mysterious potency. *So shall my Word be that
goeth out of My mouth: it shall not return unto me void, but it
shall accomplish that which I please, and it shall prosper in the
thing whereto I sent it* (Isaiah 55:11, A.V.). There may be less
distance than we thought to be traversed between that and the
fourth Gospel: *In the beginning was the Word, and the Word
was with God, and the Word was God* (John 1:1, A.V.). Or
this: *Heaven and earth shall pass away: but my words shall
not pass away* (Mark 13:31, A.V.). There are things writ in
water, but words are not. They "toil terribly" upon human life.
The least you and I can do is to respect them. They are the only
method we have of what Dr. Farmer calls "communication
without trespass."

It will follow at once that what you have to say you will say truthfully and with precision. "Speak with moderation, but think with great fierceness." If there is anything distressing, it is to listen to a man who goes on about something, runs off into little inaccuracies, comes back with an exaggeration, and winds up in an atmosphere of frenzied inadequacy. After a while people lose confidence even in his moral integrity! *I do not falsify the word of God,* writes Paul (II Corinthians 4:2).

I State the Truth Openly

*and so commend myself to every man's conscience before God: a man of sincerity* (2:17). Consider the almost startling effectiveness of a little exactitude in this passage which C. E. Montague lifts from a sermon by Jowett of Oxford:

He never, as some preachers did, put in to two hundred healthy young men, as a quite likely thing, that they might die in the next night and have to give to God, about breakfast-time, an account of their stewardships. Neither did he suggest, as other preachers did, that they were all going to live to be threescore and ten. What he said was, "I find it set down in tables that the average duration of human life at the age of twenty-one is about thirty-six years. We may hope for a little more; we may fear a little less; but, speaking generally, thirty-six years, or about 13,000 days, is the time in which our task must be accomplished." For myself and some others, . . . I can testify this: Our young minds were as electrified by this quaint piece of precision, so unexpected from a pulpit, that they were instantly opened wide for the reception of what followed—that we should be shabby fellows if we spent any serious proportion of our 13,000 days in shirking or whining or sponging on the more manful part of mankind.[8]

By way of contrast, here is a distinguished lecturer on preaching carried away by his zeal as he undertakes to describe the ideal pastor: "He ministers from morning until even and far on into the night at that altar of God which the heart of man is." It is good poetry, but it is tremendously poor fact. And nobody could possibly come away from it with it with anything but a vague sense of words that have been hollowed out on the inside and filled with whipped cream. And here is another writing of his own spiritual and mental habits: "What I consider most important is the continual thought that is going on in my mind which constitutes my real preparation for the pulpit. . . . I am always thinking about religious things." And with that he and I parted company. It may have been true for him. I hope so. It failed so far of being true in my case that what business the two of us had to transact thereafter had to be done by parcel post with foreign postage.

If I may be allowed another personal reminiscence at this point, I can still go back to the moment when at the close of a beautiful service I found myself being swept along irresistibly by the wings of a glorious prayer. Then suddenly I was on the earth with a thud. Without being in any mood to cavil, I had instinctively recoiled from the petition, "Take from our hearts, O God, all hypocrisy." Now that simply is not done. After one of the most searching addresses I had ever heard, I just could not ask for any such messianic issue. Standing as we all had been for those dear moments under the blinding light of God's holiness, I scarcely wanted what this man was praying for, so distant was it from my soul. Truth must still remain truth. Let it dwell in "the spare and vivid precision of thoroughbred speech."[9] Never try to make it puissant by stepping it up and so turning it into a lie. Lies may travel a mile while truth is putting on its boots; but nobody likes the place lies take them!

There is more than that, however, still to be said. From a psychological point of view you may even have an immoderate emphasis on the truth itself. It remains truth, no doubt of that, but there is almost too much of it to be anything short of funny. Not long ago a great crowd of us listened to a popular minister delivering an address on The Morals of America. He began by piling one statistic on another. Then oratory jumped in, followed by some more statistics and some more oratory. Unquestionably the facts were above reproach; but I found myself pretty soon in the mood of the Queen in *Alice in Wonderland,* who set herself for half an hour each morning the task of believing what was not so. A preacher so easily becomes the victim of his own enthusiasms. There are even times, I am afraid, when by our violent denunciation we actually create a market for the things we berate. Somewhat like the priest in Ireland who is quoted as having said, "It's whiskey that's the bane of this congregation. It's whiskey that steals away a man's brains. It's whiskey that makes you shoot at landlords and miss them!" It would be interesting to know how many pious folk, after listening to a sermon against cards or drink or motion pictures, drop their knitting for a moment, figuratively speaking, and ask themselves secretly with a sigh how it would feel to be just a little wicked.

Say what you have to say truthfully. Then say what you have to say simply. A shorter word is almost always better than a longer. *The London Times* is cited as having preserved a priceless sentence from the homily of a most distinguished divine in which he reminded the simple folk of the Lake Country where Wordsworth used to live that they were surrounded by "an apodeiksis of theopratic omnipotence."[10] And I dare say the poor souls being thus surrounded were cut off from all retreat! One finds in all great writing a simplicity which is the very acme of art, the last word in decoration, the *simplex munditiis* of Horace, unpretentious elegance: the huge simplicity of such words as grace and love and faith and sin and hope and death. Did you ever count over on your fingers the amazing number of God's one-syllabled immensities? Though, may I add, I should not overuse them. Most of them need careful definition. People do not know what grace is, what faith is, what sin is. They are such simple words that nobody much does any business with them. They fall "flat like tombstones over dead ideas." Tell your congregation what they mean; but do it with simplicity, with the simplicity of the Lord's Prayer or of those quiet words of Jesus: *Come unto me, all ye that labour and are heavy laden, and I will give you rest. Take my yoke upon you, and learn of me, for I am meek and lowly of heart: and ye shall find rest unto your souls. For my yoke is easy, and my burden is light.* (Matthew 11:28–30, A.V.) As Adam Philip has pointed out, there are fifty-two words there, and only nine of them are of more than one syllable. Or again: *Behold, I stand at the door, and knock: if any man hear my voice, and open the door, I will come in to him, and will sup with him, and he with me* (Revelation 3:20, A.V.). It is the simplicity with which all majesty clothes itself.

Third, my counsel would be to say what you have to say pictorially. Follow that through these letters of Paul some time. I believe we can manage it. It can be done by exchanging the commonplace phrase, the torpid, sluggish word, for words that glow and move and have some being, leaving those that lie down on the page with their four legs in the air, panting out their life, for others that gird their loins to run and not be weary, to walk and not faint. "You may use words," to quote C. E. Montague again, "as a means of approach to life's burning heart, or as sheets of asbestos, fire-proof doors to put up between you and those central flames."[11] Never if you can help it, very rarely at most, use the word "thing," or that other word "great." Be specific. Say what thing you mean, and say how great it is. Watch the crystallizations and precipitates in a passage like this. It is a comment by G. K. Chesterton on the Sinclair Lewis or Henry Mencken type of rebel against the so-called "Victorian decencies":

He describes a world which appears to be a dull and discoloring illusion of indigestion, not bright enough to be called a nightmare; smelly but not even stinking with any strength; smelling of the staleness of ignorant chemical experiments by dirty, secretive schoolboys—the sort of boys who torture cats in corners; spineless and spiritless like a broken-backed worm; loathsomely slow and laborious like an endless slug; despairing, but not with dignity; blaspheming, but not with courage; without wit, without will, without laughter or uplifting of heart; too old to die, too deaf to leave off talking; too blind to stop; too stupid to start afresh, too dead to be killed, and incapable of being damned.[12]

That is hardly writing; it is painting. Here it is in Phillips Brooks' sermon, The Mind's Love for God: "When the procession of your powers goes up joyfully singing to worship in the temple, do not leave the noblest of them all behind to cook the dinner and to tend the house." It is the kind of craftsmanship of which Confucius once said, "A picture is worth a thousand words." It is the attempt to make men see, to "turn their ears into eyes," as Dr. Coffin once put it. Watch it in Browning as he has Andrea del Sarto, "the faultless painter," murmur to himself of others, of Raphael and Michelangelo, poorer yet richer than he:

> There burns a truer light of God in them,
> In their vexed, beating, stuffed and stopped-up brains,
> Heart, or whate'er else, than goes on to prompt
> This low-pulsed forthright craftsman's hand of mine.
> Their works drop groundward, but themselves, I know,
> Reach many a time a heaven that's shut to me,
> Enter and take their place there, sure enough,
> Though they come back and cannot tell the world.
> My works are nearer Heaven, but I sit here.

Or take this, for movement: "Every heart vibrates to that iron string." See what a difference the word "iron" makes in the force and almost audible twang of the sentence. Recall, if you will, Faber's phrase descriptive of childhood's God: "A tingling silence in the room." Sometimes the very rhythm and flow of words suffice to leave an indelible picture on the mind. Read Milton, in *Paradise Lost,* describing the towering yet tragic figure of Satan:

As when the sun new-risen
Looks through the horizontal, misty air,
Shorn of his beams, or from behind the moon
In dim eclipse, disastrous twilight sheds
On half the nations, and with fear of change
Perplexes monarchs.[13]

Here is vividness of detail, here is the color of adjectives, not splashed about with a prodigal hand, but hoarded as a miser hoards his gold and lets it trickle through his fingers. Here is the swiftness of verbs. You can come upon the same thing on almost any page of the New Testament, especially in the Vulgate: *And there shall be signs in the sun, and in the moon, and in the stars; and upon the earth distress of nations, with perplexity; the sea and the waves roaring; men's hearts failing them for fear, and for looking after those things which are coming on the earth* . . . (Luke 21:25, 26, A.V.). Or this: *For I am persuaded, that neither death, nor life, nor angels, nor principalities, nor powers, nor things present, nor things to come, nor height, nor depth, nor any other creature, shall be able to separate us from the love of God, which is in Christ Jesus our Lord* (Romans 8:38, 39, A.V.).

"Ah, but," you say, "all that is quite beyond me." I do not believe it. I do not believe it is quite beyond any of us. May I make here one attempt of my own simply to show you what I mean when I keep urging you to some honest effort in the direction of concreteness, movement, color, life; when I keep insisting that it is not enough just to say what there is to say and have done, that you must say it alive!

Let me suppose that the subject again is Nicodemus. You want to picture his bewildered uncertainties, his broken responses, his quick recoil. It may run something like this: "Jesus haunted Nicodemus; that was one thing. And dreams haunted him; that was another. He did not want to lose anything if he could help it. He did not like the idea of what people would say about him. He was a little too old, too lacking in the spirit of adventure, to relish starting out on a new and an untried course. But he could not sit still where he was any longer. He had a few visions left of all that he had seen once. Comfort was not everything. There was a life to live that a man could yearn toward for its beauty, and other lives to tend, throwing a little loveliness around them like the fold of a cloak hanging from your arm. He could not sit still any longer and keep saying to himself that nothing could be done about it, that he would have to put up with it as it was. You had to edge on a little toward love, and mercy, and brotherhood, and the Kingdom of God. If you did not, you could not sleep. Things got hold of you by the elbow and caught you round the feet and tried to hold you back, but you had to move. The eyes of this man from Nazareth, or his hands, or the queer things he said—pictures, echoes, furtive hopes—what was it? Something. You had to move. So is it written: *There was a man of the Pharisees, named Nicodemus, a ruler of the Jews: the same came to Jesus by night."* (John 3:1, 2, A.V.) Do you see? That comes far from achieving what it sets out to do: but it may give you some little hint and encouragement perhaps; some suggestion of that aliveness which all writing, to be effective, must in one way or another at least attempt.

My fourth word of counsel is that you say what you have to say with clarity. *If the trumpet sounds indistinct, who will get ready for the fray? . . . Unless your tongue utters*

Language That Is Readily Understood

*how can people make out what you say? You will be pouring words into the empty air! There are ever so many kinds of language in the world, every one of them meaning something. Well, unless I understand the meaning of what is said to me, I shall appear to the speaker to be talking gibberish, and to my mind he will be talking gibberish himself. . . . I would rather say five words*

*with my own mind . . . than ten thousand words in a "tongue."*
So Paul, writing in that vigorous way of his about the gift of
tongues, cutting knots where it would take too long to untie
them (I Corinthians 14:8–12, 19). *You don't have to read between the lines of my letters,* he adds later on (II Corinthians
1:13); *you can understand them.* In his far less dignified fashion, Sam Jones once put it: "I aim to spread fodder right out on
the ground, where anything from a giraffe to a jackass can get
at it."

There are sermons, though, where this business of clarity is
overdone. Montague in one place suggests that all of us, at some
time or other, must have

. . . groaned dumbly under a flood of clearness from a pulpit. First
the giving out of a text, clear as noon, perhaps the words "A City that
is Set on a Hill Cannot be Hid." Then the illumination of this
heavenly lamp by setting out, all round it, pound after pound of
tallow candles. From word to word of the text the hapless divine
straggles onward, matchbox in hand . . . till the martyred Christian below has to ask, in his heart, Shall I never hit back? . . .
It is one way of hymning, with a pious and complacent humility,
one's freedom from intellectual baggage: Nothing in my brain I
bring. . . . A courteous writer even in his most explicit moments
will stop short of rubbing into our minds the last item of all he
means. He will make us wrestle with him a little in the dark before
he yields his full meaning, as God made the patriarch wrestle with
the angel, to the patriarch's ultimate advantage. . . . He will edge
you into the right corner, put the pie within reach, then withdraw
gently and leave you to put in your thumb and pull out a plum
and think what a bright boy or girl you are. He will know how
much more blessed it is for a reader to guess right than to be told!

I myself know of one minister who for twenty years has been
leaning over backward toward "the honest and the explicit."
For that long he has ruthlessly confined himself to words of
two syllables at most, so he has told me. And I think of the people whom Saki (H. H. Monro) so amusingly describes. They
prefer a picture

. . . that tells its own story, with generous assistance from the title. A riderless war horse with harness in obvious disarray, straggling into a courtyard full of pale, swooning women, and marginally noted "bad news," suggests to their minds a distinct interpretation of some military catastrophe. They can see what it was meant to convey and explain it to friends of duller intelligence.

Nevertheless, and for all that and all that, a sermon cannot do much good if only a few people can take it in. Never consciously preach down to what you believe the level of any congregation. That level may be a good deal higher than you think. Even if it is not, preaching down to it is an egotistic, supercilious, and insulting thing to do, whether you are talking to coal miners, or children, or just plain bankers. Make a habit of preaching up toward your subject and you will be safer. But see that it is clear. Said Principal Denney: "The man who shoots above the target does not prove thereby that he has superior ammunition. He just proves that he can't shoot!"[14] We have to school ourselves rigidly in the fine art of being understood. You will allow me to speak feelingly, being cursed myself with what some people say is a sort of knack for words and phrases, and liking them so well that I have been known more than once to lay a sentence down on an altar to the picturesque and without more ado cut its throat.

Of course, there will be somebody in your congregation on a given Sunday who is bound not to get much out of anything. These folk have been up too late the night before or they have had too many hot-cakes for breakfast. I remember preaching once in my cousin's church in Richmond on The Risk of Prayer. The point was that true praying really involved a set of rather genuine hazards. For one thing there was the danger of seeing yourself as you are; and for another there was the danger of becoming more like Jesus, as the old song has it, like Jesus in a world which crucified him and would do it again. I thought all this was not just a prospect to be viewed with composure. After the service a dear soul, a member of the congregation, came up to my cousin, her pastor, and said, "Well, Dr. Scherer, I can't help what your relative from New York says! I'm going right on praying!" There is not a great deal that can be done about such things. You may be quite lucid and find that here or there some receiving apparatus is out of order, as was the case with the three slightly deaf Englishmen on the train from London. It came crawling into a station, and one called to another, "Is this Wembley?" "No," answered the second, "it's Thursday!" Whereupon the third chimed in, "I am too; let's get something to drink!" You cannot see to it that the minds in front of you are ready and receptive; but you can see to it that your sermon is not so bedecked with rhetoric that the pattern of it is lost, that nowhere in the course of it have you "mounted the horse, obscurity, to escape the dragon, nonsense!"[15]

You can see to it that the ideas in your own mind are not chaotic and confused, as were hers who averred that she never knew what she thought until she had heard what she said. You can see to it that they are not ill wrought out. You can see to it that your matter is well ordered, and that there is no lack of emphasis on vital points. It used to be bandied about at the seminary that every sermon should consist of only three divisions: First, you tell the congregation what points you are going to make; then you make them; and finally you tell them what points you have made. It is not altogether ridiculous. If we who are preachers had a little more experience listening to sermons, we would understand that listening is not so easy. At our last national convention I asked two ministers what another had said,—they had told me that his sermon was so impressive. And neither of them could give me more than the barest outline! It was the impact of life upon life that meant most to them. I used to think, too, that that meant most. I do not believe now that the impact of a few ideas clearly expressed and a truth or two driven firmly home hurts any.

The point to remember is that even with our preparation and background and normal interest, listening is not easy. It is an art, and it has to be acquired. I should undertake if I were you to train my people in it—pupils of the church school, members of the confirmation class. But you must always make allowance for the difficulties. Write them down as your major premise. You know what you are going to say next Sunday; it is clear to you. But how many others who have given it no thought, who hear the sentences spoken but once, who are assaulted by every kind of disturbance, the noises outside, the woman in front, the usher at the end of the pew, the little girl with a cough—how many others will know what you have said when you have said it? Go over your sermon again Saturday morning, thinking of them. You do want to help them, don't you? Very well. Start by rooting up the mixed metaphors. One lad said in his sermon on Marriage, "The ship of wedded love will founder unless it is grounded on a rock!" And he concluded, "So live that at the last you may say with the apostle, 'I have fought a good fight!'" Then lop off all the decorating you have done for decoration's sake. Take out the words that hinder. After that, take out the words that don't help. Get your Roget's *Thesaurus* and find others that will give things a push.

Make it clearer at the outset what it is you mean to do. Look at the end of each paragraph and the beginning of the next. Are the transitions clearly made? Glancing back over my own sermons in their typed form, I find that the hand-written additions I worked in just before preaching them had to do almost entirely with the effort to make those transitions clearer. Is it obvious what you are about, what you have completed, what you are beginning, whence you have come and whither you are going? Read those last and first sentences of each paragraph again, and remember that you must sustain what you have to say, not just drop one point to pick up another. Then watch the phrases you particularly like, and with a bloody axe chop them away if they make no real contribution, until you can feel that what is left may really do something worth while.

It is quite possible that some even of that needs to be rewritten. If you have made the first copy in pencil, the rewriting is not hard to do. Scarcely ever will all of it go into the Saturday morning mill and come out just the same. My Saturday mind shakes its head with considerable regularity at the way my Friday mind was operating and proceeds to check that culprit's weird and often unconscious motions. There does, indeed, seem to be an underlying pattern controlling them, much as there is in sleep-walking; but it is usually no more than a kind of creation heaving through the chaos. Sometimes on Saturday morning God says, *Let there be light,* and sometimes there is. Things occasionally spring to attention like soldiers. The introduction becomes the first head; the first head, the third; the third, the second; while the second tears itself out of the middle and stands up at the very beginning.

Whatever happens, when you are done, if you have a patient wife, read it to her. Perhaps it would be well to read it to her first, maybe as early as Friday evening, so that you may have her verdict on hand for the Saturday morning revision. And for your sake I hope she is hard on you; that while everybody else adores you, she will cast down her quiet eyes now and then whimsically at your feet of clay. I bear grateful witness in my more objective and un-self-conscious moods that if anybody can save you, a wife can,—or a not too fatuous mother.

And over it all, let me insist, over it all pray God there shall brood some sense of the Infinite; beyond everything that you say, towering suggestions, as if you had not been able quite to tell what you had seen or to recount all that you had heard. You are to speak

## The Mysterious Wisdom of God*

Let it have its height and its horizons. Never, as another has put it, never go to the brim of that great ocean which God is, dip your tumbler into it and, setting the tumbler down before your people, say, "There; there is the ocean!"[16] "Language," writes Joad, "is significant only if it is able to indicate something beyond language."

"Say nothing that is too small to be true" is the urgent word of Dr. Farmer; "nothing too confident to be true; nothing too easy to be true!"[17] "I like lucidity," declares Denney, "as much as anyone; but I like still better the sense of magnitude and even of immensity in a man dealing with revealed religion." Ruskin once wrote of Turner that in a square inch of his skies you could find the Infinite.[18] "I burn," says Emerson, "after the *aliquid immensum infinitumque.*"[19] What you are after, says Jowett, is not that folk shall say at the end of it all, "What an excellent sermon!" That is a measured failure. You are there to have them say, when it is over, "What a great God!" It is something for men not to have been in your presence but in His.

In my childhood's home there was a great conch from the Gulf of Mexico, which years before had been used to call the farm-hands to their meals. The point of it had been filed off, and, grasping it firmly with one hand, a good, stout fellow could put it to his lips and sound a withering blast. But what intrigued me most was the low and ceaseless roar you could hear if you held it to your ear. They told me, as they have told you, that it was the roar of the distant waves shut up within those twisted chambers, down the winding corridors of the shell. I want to hear in the sermons a man preaches, in his poor orphaned words,—I want to hear forever the sound of the prisoned sea.

\* I Corinthians 2:7.

And now, shall we say, it is Sunday morning, and you are about to go into the pulpit with that sermon of yours. I have in front of me as I go into the chancel what has for many years gone incorrectly by the name of Luther's Sacristy Prayer. It serves me well.

Lord God, Father in Heaven, I am altogether unworthy of the office and service wherein I am to publish Thy glory and nourish and tend this congregation. But since Thou hast appointed me to be a shepherd and to teach the Word, and since the people also are in need of the teaching and instruction, so be my Helper and let Thy holy angel be with me. Let it please Thee through me to accomplish something to Thy glory and not to mine, or to the praise of men; and so bestow upon me of Thy manifest grace and mercy, a right understanding of Thy Word; and far more be pleased that I may also do it. Jesus Christ, Son of the Living God, Shepherd and Bishop of our souls, send thy Holy Spirit to be with me in this work; yea to work in me thy will and purpose through thy divine power. Amen.

Here is Bernard Iddings Bell, writing of his practice before the opening of the service:

I shall get down on my knees; beat my breast—inconspicuously—three times in token of my sinfulness; make the sign of the cross, in token of my Master's love; and say a prayer, which always goes about like this: "God, this sermon is not much good, but I have worked honestly at it and it is the best I can do right now. If it is to do any good at all, it is You Who will do that good and not I. Please use me in my sermon as best You can. I love You and I love these people. That's that. Amen."[20]

Such praying will not minister to you any great amount of self-confidence. If there is anything in you at all, you will go on being nervous. You will never get over that anticipatory restlessness and unease. But honest men do find a faithful God Who to His eternal glory stands them on their feet with

## Full Power to Speak*

So, at long last, as it will seem to your bound and eager spirit, having, for all the straining of your desire, schooled yourself to quiet worship, perhaps under the trailing majesties of some ancient ritual, you climb the steps of the pulpit and take your place before the waiting people whom God for that high hour has entrusted to you. It is in this moment that the week for you is at its summit. How, then, shall you deliver the sermon which you have so earnestly wrought?

I think it will help perhaps more than anything else to remember what purpose is yours in coming. May I give you Dr. Jowett's setting of it?

It is our God-appointed office to lead men and women who are weary or wayward, exultant or depressed, eager or indifferent, into "the secret place of the Most High." We are to help the sinful to the fountain of cleansing, the bond slaves to the wonderful songs of deliverance. We are to help the halt and the lame to recover their lost nimbleness. We are to help the broken-winged into the healing light of "the heavenly places in Christ Jesus." We are to help the sad into the sunshine of grace. We are to help the buoyant to clothe themselves with "the garment of praise." We are to help redeem the strong from the atheism of pride and the weak from the atheism of despair. We are to help little children see the glorious attractiveness of God, and we are to help the aged realize the encompassing care of the Father and the assurance of the eternal home.[21]

I have wanted for some time to do in parchment for my sacristy the words of M. J. McLeod:

To speak that we know and testify that we have seen, to speak it lovingly, to testify it boldly, never seeking to raise doubts, ever aiming to kindle faith and hope; to be receptive in the study, an empty vessel sanctified and waiting to be filled from the ever-open fountain, then in the pulpit to aim to take of this fullness and shew it into others; not primarily to proclaim a doctrine but rather to tell

* I Corinthians 1:5.

a story, to tell how it has affected our own lives; to have as the heart's desire the longing to give our people a taste of some precious blessing that we have found ourselves in the secret place; never to be trifling or self-advertising, ever to be tremendously in earnest and when possible at all, self-effacing; to bathe in the Book till it enters into the very texture of our speech. To love men, to be moved with a great pity at their presence, to see not merely a sea of faces, but rather a company of spirits, to compel their ears, to touch their consciences; never to allow ourselves to be turned aside to wrangle, negation or debate, to avoid technicalities and trivial things, to magnify the certainties and things of vital moment; to lift up Jesus to the eyes of men, to proclaim His love, His forgiveness, His cleansing power, His joy, His hope, His glory; thus to create in our listeners a hunger for holy living by backing up a great message with a great, noble, loving life.

There are the knowledge that comes at first-hand, the stewardship of it, the witnessing, the humility, the compassion, the Christ-centeredness, which alone can give a man his sense of high appointment. Once understand that, and there will be little trouble with the delivery. It will not be stilted and self-conscious, it will not be violent or sensational, it will not be studied and theatrical, it will not be trifling or smart; it will be distinct but not loud, in a voice flexible, yet sturdy enough to keep out of that pernicious tail-spin at the end of every other sentence which leaves half the congregation gasping for the verb; it will be straightforward and earnest and kindly; it will be a "pleading with men," an effort to persuade them, under the shadow of the Almighty, pressing them on toward that love *which springs from a pure heart, from a good conscience, and from a sincere faith* (I Timothy, 1:5). "Whether with the bow or the stick, once wrote *The London Observer* of Pablo Casals, cellist, conductor, composer, "he plays as if he held a responsible trust, determined that at all costs the purity of the faith shall not suffer at his hands. He refrains from anything histrionic or ephemeral; he wants the truth of it. . . . In whatever he does he seems to aim at some invisible and unattainable ideal."[22]

May I say at once that the manuscript, if you take it with you, should not be read? You remember the old Scottish woman and her three criticisms of a sermon: "It was read, it was no' well read, it was no' worth reading!" You may possibly drive people by reading to them; but you will not lead them that way. Reading is far too impersonal a method for the pulpit. And I say this, being quite aware the while that some of the world's greatest preachers always read; notably, perhaps, Chalmers and Phillips Brooks. Among the living, James Black not infrequently does it in his second service. Of course, these men could read, and James Black is still in the present tense. You would see little difference between his reading and another man's free delivery. On the whole, however, it is by no means a practice to be commended. Somehow, if you are going to have a manuscript with you at all, you must be both its slave and its master. I mean you must know it well enough to transmit its excellencies of thought and order and expression; and at the same time you must stand by it lightly enough to be in quick command of the situation should you wish to make any sudden additions, to take advantage of the wealth which the Spirit of God will sometimes open up before you even as you speak. As for me, I must either use the barest of notes, or I must deliver what I have written pretty much word for word. Anywhere between the two I am apt to be lost.

I should not call my usual method *memoriter*, because it does not bind me to the process of recalling; but after two or three hours with my manuscript on Saturday afternoon, with a hasty review on Sunday morning, I can if I wish preach letter-perfect what I have written. I do not suggest that you adopt my method, or any man's, though indeed I have heard many preachers who I wished might try writing and memorizing. You must discover your own way of doing it best. Try them all, and do not just choose the easiest; choose the most effective.

But whatever you do, whether you take with you into the

pulpit what you have written or lay it aside, whether you cultivate the art of unobtrusive reading or the art of free delivery,
memoriter or otherwise, give yourself wholly in that thirty
minutes. Learn to forget everything but your message, and the
God Whose truth it is, and the people who sit there needing it,
and the love you have for them. Let it be done urgently and
warmly and calmly, as a friend would speak with his friend.
My own habit is to begin with a sentence prayer and to close
with another. I think I shall always continue it.

In any case, never begin with heat or on a high note. You
will blow up somewhere in the middle if you do, with the last
ten minutes reserved for the falling of pieces over the landscape. From end to end keep your emotions under control; not
under a bushel, mind you—under control. There are times
when they ought to show. *Ardeat orator qui vult accendere
populum,* in the words of Quintilian. If you ever want to set
anybody on fire, you have to burn a little yourself. It was said
recently in my hearing that a certain preacher always seems to
pick up his subject here and set it down there; but he himself is
never behind it. Be sure, though, that you never get out in front
of it either and try to fight people into righteousness and love
and peace. You want to send them away in the firm and tender
hold of God, not all black and blue and exhausted and resent-
ful. They may upon occasion, indeed must, be made to feel, as
a certain devout layman put it, after hearing one of the sharp sermons of a century or more ago at quarterly communion, "To-
night Jerusalem was searched through with lanterns."[23] But they
must feel that the man with the lantern is a man with a great
love in his heart. It was with bitter tears that Paul wrote his first
letter to the church at Corinth. Be as sharp as you please with the
wrong they do, but be gentle with people always; every one of
them has a battle to fight. Encourage them in it. Do not take out
your ill humor on them or reflect in your sermon or in your bearing the misfortunes and disappointments of the week.

Such gestures as you use will come naturally to you. You will not force them or keep bringing out the same old stock Sunday after Sunday. You will, I hope, fight every distracting mannerism as you would fight the devil, and flee from it. One preacher I know snorts; another keeps his hand in front of his face, tweaking his own nose or ruffling his hair. Another points and shakes his finger. A very little bit of that goes an amazingly long way.

Avoid such words as "finally" and "lastly" and "in conclusion." As Hutton suggests, they only call attention to the lapse of time, and make everybody quite sure the whole thing was entirely too long. Besides, when you throw in the second or third "finally," the congregation begins to lose confidence in you. Dodge interjections and such exclamatory remarks as "Oh, my brethren!" and "Dearly beloved!" The simple pronoun "you" is an adequate substitute.

And I suppose you will allow me to add this: Watch your vocal chords. If you habitually shout or pitch your tones in too high or too low a key, the day may come when you shall have to pay for it, as I did, with enforced silence. And your congregation may not like that. Congregations do not all know when they are blest. In short, be your honest self, with this to be marked by everyone who hears you: that somewhere, somehow about you, there is a "naked intent stretching toward God."

May He bless you now in all your ministry. You will never let it pall on you, will you? It is far too great a thing for that. I love those words of Francis Drake when he stood on the Isthmus of Panama and got his first glimpse of the Pacific. He cried aloud, "Almighty God, of Thy goodness give me life and leave to sail once in an English ship upon that sea!"[24] You will find that there is a mercy on the long and outward voyage which tops even the promises of God! *Faithful is* He *Who called you to this fellowship with his Son Jesus Christ our Lord* (I Corinthians 1:9).

# Notes

*✦✦✦✦*

## A CONSTANT PAGEANT

NOTE

1  J. H. Jowett, *The Preacher, His Life and Work*, pp. 13–19.
2  See the ninth, tenth, and eleventh chapters of Romans.
3  This conviction permeates the thought of Hulme, Barth, Brunner, Berdyaev, Reinhold Niebuhr. Cf. especially the last named in *Nature and Destiny of Man,* p. 148, *et passim,* Charles Scribner's Sons, New York, 1941.
4  See William Ernest Hocking, *What Man Can Make of Man,* Harper & Brothers, New York, 1942.
5  April 2, 1942.
6  Spengler identified our century as the end of one of those ever-repeated cycles of culture and civilization through which the soul plods on from some new birth to old age, from spring to winter, when the fires die out, and humanity looks back piteously: weary, reluctant, cold, losing its desire to be, fondly wishing itself out of the over-long daylight back in the grave again, which is the dark womb of its mother earth (*The Decline of the West,* p. 108, Alfred A. Knopf, New York, 1932). More recently Sorokin of Harvard has discarded these sad reminiscences of a lost childhood and thinks rather that we are passing abruptly and by way of inevitable catastrophe from an epoch which was dominated by the transient and the phenomenal into another when men shall again respond, though only after the bitterest calamities and under the most desperate urgencies, to the absolutes of eternity and of God. His most recent books are *The Crisis of Our Age* and *Man and Society in Calamity,* E. P. Dutton & Company, Inc., New York. See also Arnold J. Toynbee, *A Study of History,* Oxford University Press, London, 1934–39, for an analysis of the rise and fall of civilizations.

7 See Thomas Woodlock, *The Catholic Pattern,* Part Two, Simon and Schuster, New York, 1942.

8 Berdyaev, *The End of Our Time,* p. 80, Eng. trans.

9 *The Philosophical Aspects of Modern Science,* The Macmillan Company, New York, 1932.

10 See Chapter 3 of these lectures.

11 Frederick W. H. Myers, *St. Paul—Collected Poems,* The Macmillan Company, New York.

12 *The Glory of the Ministry,* p. 7, Fleming H. Revell Company, New York.

13 Francis Thompson, *The Hound of Heaven.*

14 Hutton, *That the Ministry Be Not Blamed,* p. 120.

15 This is reminiscent of something I believe which Dr. Fosdick has said. Certainly he illustrates it.

16 Quoted by Jowett, *op. cit.,* p. 103.

CHAPTER II

LIKE A MAN OF GOD

1 See Kenneth Kirk, *The Vision of God.*

2 Quoted from *The Abingdon Bible Commentary,* p. 759.

3 *The Christian News-Letter,* Dec. 30, 1942.

4 This was Massilon's remark to one who congratulated him on his sermons. Scott, *Preaching Week by Week,* p. 156, Hodder & Stoughton, Ltd., London.

5 Burnet, *Pleading with Men,* p. 178, Fleming H. Revell Company, New York, 1935.

6 Quoted by Robertson, *The Glory of the Ministry,* p. 27.

7 *The Expositor's Bible,* p. 171, Armstrong & Son, 1901.

8 John Masefield, "The Seekers," from *Poems,* The Macmillan Company, New York, 1923.

9 Kinloch, *Village Sermons by a Novelist,* pp. 25 f., D. Appleton-Century Company, Inc., New York, 1924.

10 T. E. Brown, quoted by Arthur John Gossip in *The Galilean Accent,* p. 194, T. & T. Clark, Edinburgh.

11 *Jesus Came Preaching,* Charles Scribner's Sons, New York, 1936, p. 210.

12  From a memorandum on "Preaching as an Expression of the Ethical Reality of the Church" by the Chicago Ecumenical Group. Address John C. Bennett, Union Theological Seminary, New York.

13  Robertson, *op. cit.,* p. 192.

14  *Purity of Heart,* pp. 198 f., Harper & Brothers, New York, 1938.

# CHAPTER III

THE WEAPONS OF MY WARFARE

1  Adam Philip, *Thoughts on Worship and Preaching,* p. 130, James Clarke & Co., Ltd., London.

2  Matthew 22:40, A.V. Cited by John Oman, *Concerning the Ministry,* p. 165, Harper & Brothers, New York, 1937.

3  *Parnassus on Wheels.*

4  Adam Philip, *op. cit.*

5  *The Christian Faith,* pp. 79–80, Harper & Brothers, New York, 1942.

6  Joseph Fort Newton, *If I Had Only One Sermon to Prepare,* p. 49, Harper & Brothers, New York, 1932.

7  J. H. Jowett, *The Preacher, His Life and Work,* p. 97.

8  *Religion in Our Times,* p. 126.

9  *God's Search for Man,* translated by George W. Richards *et al.,* pp. 29, 30, 49, Round Table Press, 1935.

10  Read on this point E. W. Barnes, *Scientific Theory and Religion,* pp. 612, 613, New York, 1933; quoted in *The Logic of Belief,* by Trueblood, Harper & Brothers, New York, 1942, p. 279.

11  See his review of *The Spiritual Life,* by Edgar Sheffield, *The Christian Century,* p. 1216, Oct. 7, 1942.

12  *The New York Times,* Feb. 19, 1943.

13  Dixon, *The Human Situation,* p. 143.

14  *Social Salvation,* pp. 185, 186.

15  From "The Marshes of Glynn," by Sidney Lanier.

16  Quoted, *Sermons, An Augustine Synthesis,* arranged by Erich Przywara, p. 298, Sheed & Ward, Inc., New York, 1936.

17 Fosdick, *A Guide to Understanding the Bible,* Harper & Brothers, 1938; pp. 95, 96.

18 *Our Eternal Contemporory,* pp. 105, 106, Harper & Brothers, New York, 1942.

19 *The Nature and Destiny of Man,* Vol. 1, pp. 24, 94 ff.

20 See I Corinthians 15:1–11 for a summary of this gospel.

21 See *Christendom,* Summer 1942, p. 365; article by Prof. Widgery of Duke University.

22 See Carlton, *Shakespearian Comedy.*

23 Robert Browning, "Prospice."

24 See Matthew's account.

25 By Lenore Coffee and William Joyce Corven.

26 *Macbeth,* Act V, Scene 5.

27 *Hamlet,* Act V, Scene 1.

CHAPTER IV

GOD APPEALING BY ME

1 Farmer, *The Servant of the Word,* p. 89, Chas. Scribner's Sons, New York, 1942.

2 *The Christian Faith,* p. 59, Harper & Brothers, 1942.

3 Edward Rowland Sill, "The Reformer."

4 Quoted by Oxnam, *Preaching and the Social Crisis,* p. 160.

5 Professor G. van de Leeuw; see note 8 below.

6 From a memorandum on "Preaching as the Expression of the Ethical Reality of the Church" by the Chicago Ecumenical Group, paragraph 46.

7 *The Atlantic,* Oct., 1942, p. 112.

8 "European Preaching in Wartime," *Information Service,* vol. xxii, No. 3.

9 Nels Ferré, *The Christian Faith,* p. 64.

10 William Ernest Hocking, *The Meaning of God in Human Experience.*

11 Recorded in *While Rome Burns.*

12 "Abt Vogler," stanza 7.

13 *The Man Born to Be King;* quoted by Robert Searle in *Tell It to the Padre,* p. 65, Farrar & Rinehart, Inc., New York, 1943.

14 J. H. Jowett, *The Preacher, His Life and Work,* p. 99.

15  Burnet, *Pleading with Men*, p. 165.
16  From words of Denney, quoted by Burnet, *op. cit.*, p. 102.
17  Adam Philip, *Thoughts on Worship and Preaching*, p. 102.
18  Jowett, *op. cit.*, p. 147.
19  Dwight Bradley. Quoted by Bowie in *Which Way Ahead?*, p. 28, Harper & Brothers, New York, 1943.

CHAPTER V

A SOUND WORKMAN

1  Read I Corinthians 1:17 ff. and 2:1 ff.
2  Quoted by John Oman, *Concerning the Ministry*, p. 117.
3  Adam Philip, *Thoughts on Worship and Preaching*.
4  *That the Ministry Be Not Blamed*, George H. Doran Company, New York, 1921.
5  Jowett, *The Preacher, His Life and Work*, p. 121.
6  Paul Moody.
7  See Chapter III.
8  "Shakespeare and Hawaii."
9  *Concerning the Ministry*, p. 140.
10  *Village Sermons*, p. 24, D. Appleton-Century Company, Inc., New York, 1942.
11  Christopher Morley, "The Haunted Bookshop."
12  Adam Philip, *op. cit.*
13  *The Presbyterian Tribune.*
14  *Concerning the Ministry*, p. 101.
15  Burnet, *Pleading with Men*, p. 127.
16  Adam Philip, *op. cit.*
17  *The Screw Tape Letters*, The Macmillan Company, New York, 1943.
18  Burnet, *op. cit.*, p. 139.
19  Quoted of Wellington in Burnet, *op. cit.*, p. 134.
20  Archbishop Whately, quoted by Adam Philip, *op. cit.*
21  Burnet, *op. cit.*, p. 137.
22  Jowett, *op. cit.*, pp. 122–124.
23  Quoted by Coffin, *What to Preach.*
24  Winifred Kirkland tells the story beautifully in *The Man of the Hour*, The Macmillan Company, New York, 1942.

CHAPTER VI

THE WAY YOU HANDLE THE WORD OF TRUTH

1   Oman, *Concerning the Ministry*, p. 86.
2   Adam Philip, *Thoughts on Worship and Preaching.*
3   *That the Ministry Be Not Blamed*, p. 179.
4   Oman, *op. cit.*, p. 163.
5   Suggested in Newton, *If I Had Only One Sermon to Prepare*,
    p. 60.
6   See I Corinthians 9:24, 26; 12:15 ff.; also, Romans 9:20.
7   Oman, *op. cit.*, p. 87.
8   Quoted by Newton, *op. cit.*, p. 10.
9   C. E. Montague, *Rough Justice.*
10  Adam Philip, *op. cit.*
11  Montague, *op. cit.*
12  Quoted by Woodlock in *The Catholic Pattern.*
13  Book I, lines 592 ff.
14  Burnet, *Pleading with Men*, p. 164.
15  Dixon, *The Human Situation*, p. 411.
16  Adam Philip, *op. cit.*, p. 131.
17  *The Healing Cross*, Introduction, pp. vi, viii, ix, Nisbet & Co.,
    Ltd.
18  Jowett, *The Preacher, His Life and Work*, p. 99.
19  Adam Philip, *op. cit.*, pp. 131, 132.
20  Quoted by Newton, *op. cit.*, p. 145.
21  *Op. cit.*, p. 146.
22  Quoted by Arnold Keller from Lillian Littlehales, *Pablo Casals.*
23  Raymond W. Albright in *The Christian Century*, Oct. 7, 1942,
    p. 1214.
24  Burnet, *op. cit.*, p. 79.